HAWTHORNE'S FAUST

*A Study
of the
Devil Archetype*

by

WILLIAM BYSSHE STEIN

1953
UNIVERSITY OF FLORIDA PRESS
Gainesville

PREFACE

UR UNDERSTANDING OF HAWTHORNE'S ART is substantially no clearer today than it was at the beginning of the twentieth century. Though modern scholars have made some progress toward a definitive biography, in their critical endeavors they have shed relatively little new light on his main narrative purpose. This fact can be explained by their bemused allegiance to traditional Hawthorne criticism. Under the spell of this school they still subscribe to the belief that he was an uneven craftsman, not averse to verbalizing the trivial and the trite. Yet a close examination of even his so-called flimsy works discloses them to be indispensable commentaries on his more serious compositions. The chief consequence of their neglect has been to foster an unwarranted deprecation of the unity of Hawthorne's total creative accomplishment. This view continues to be strengthened by innumerable anthologists whose selections betray their imitation, not their critical discrimination. As a result, the study of his techniques is invariably restricted to *The Scarlet Letter* and a narrow cross section of short stories. It is no wonder, then, that this group of tales has absorbed, if not exhausted, the energies of generation after generation of hapless students and their teachers.

This critical bias has also bred another evil — critical bookkeeping. Since, to these scholars, his art reveals no genetic development, his recurrent themes are mechanically separated and catalogued and counted. The result is inevitable. Hawthorne obviously exhibits an obsession with a line of action that centers upon the morbid conditions of the spirit. On this basis he is degraded to the station of an anachronistic Puritan who was continually brooding over the dire fatality of natural depravity. No consideration is given to the possibility that this unwavering focus on the same complex of themes represents the variations of universal human conduct in different individuals. Yet the insistence upon treating each of Hawthorne's stories as a separate entity, however much connected to others in theme, has led to the anatomization of his creative imagination. Dismembering specialists have fallen upon the corpus of his works as if it were a cadaver. After they have torn away the members toward which they incline, they have duly labeled and filed their findings according to conventional critical tastes. Ironically, they have never sought to establish the interrelations of Hawthorne's thought in his varied works. Therefore an intelligent and accurate conception of his fictional intentions has never been articulated.

This study proposes to pioneer a new path in Hawthorne criticism. It seeks to reveal the organic nature of his artistic accomplishment. Though the approach is primarily analytical, it continually moves toward a synthesis which discloses the unbroken continuity of his art and his thought, a creative impulse that asserts itself first in *Fanshawe* and still controls the narrative intention of his unfinished novels. No pretension to complete inclusiveness is advanced. However, those stories and sketches omitted from consideration are represented by others which elaborate the same theme in much the same manner. To this degree, then, this critical effort provides a full perspective on Hawthorne's artistic development, especially since the stories are examined chronologically. In addition, as a means of validating my thesis on historical grounds, the intellectual milieu of Hawthorne and his contemporaries is recreated in the opening phases of the book.

This project, like most literary undertakings, has incurred many obligations. Its timid inception and final growth owe much to Dr. Harry R. Warfel's understanding and insight. For its final form I am deeply indebted to Mr. John Parke, the assistant editor of the University of Florida Press, whose critical penetration uncovered many awkward inconsistencies in the original manuscript. To the director of the press, Dr. Lewis Francis Haines, I am obligated in countless ways, especially for his encouragement in the travail of revision. Nor can I ignore the contributions of the members of my seminar group in Hawthorne at Washington and Jefferson College, whose constant curiosity spurred me on to verify the basic premises of the study. Other persons, too numerous to mention, have been taxed for counsel and advice. But my wife, Gertrude M. Stein, commands my deepest gratitude. She has shared not only the arduous tasks of proofreading and typing, but also my own dark despair in moments when inspiration flagged.

WILLIAM BYSSHE STEIN

CONTENTS

CHAPTER I

HAWTHORNE'S FAUST MYTH

HE WHOLE AFFAIR is a manifest catchpenny!" shouts a critic at Hawthorne, bemoaning the frail pasteboard character of one of the latter's tales. —"Human art has its limits," responds the author, "and [I] must now and then ask a little aid from the [reader's] imagination." —"You will get no such aid from mine," angrily retorts the critic. "I make it a point to see things precisely as they are."[1]

This ironical exchange of opinion from a scene in Hawthorne's "Main Street" expresses the paradox of his art: a disconcertingly simple narrative pattern conceals a complex thematic substructure that conveys a multiplicity of meanings. This fictional formula places the burden of comprehension upon the reader, for the concrete details of setting, characterization, and plot reflect the deepest significance in their subtle connotations, not in their rigid denotations. But with the added difficulty of imaginative participation, this responsibility is increased. Though Hawthorne does not define the nature of the participation in the episode above, in the same story he describes it as the maintenance of "the proper point of view," an attitude of mind that transforms the objective verbal spectacle "into quite another thing." This miracle of "point of view" represents a concept of aesthetic distance. The literalist, who confuses the idealization of reality with reality itself, inevitably crowds "too near to" the pasteboard of action, thus losing "the best effect" of imaginative prose: the illusion of reality.[2]

To implement the function of Hawthorne's "point of view" the critic must assume the role of a photographer. Focusing upon the subject (the story), he must determine, according to his knowledge of the efficiency of the camera (the techniques of the author), at what distance to stand (attention to compositional details) in order to capture the nuances of light and shadow (the mutations of theme) which insure the sharpness and clarity of the photographic image (the reflection of reality). This analogy parallels Hawthorne's constant entreaties to his critics. In the preface to *Twice-Told Tales* he observes mockingly: "The book, if you would see anything in it, requires to be read in the clear, brown, twilight atmosphere in which it was written; if opened in the sunshine, it is apt to look exceedingly like a volume of blank pages."[3] The long introductory essay to *The Scarlet Letter* sounds a similar note of warning. On this occasion the tone of his reading directions is more urgent, for he couples them directly to the creative faculty. "Moonlight, in a familiar room," he insists, ". . . is a medium the most suitable for a romance-writer; . . . details . . . are so spiritualized by the unusual light, that they seem to lose their actual substance, and become things of intellect. Nothing is too small or too trifling to undergo this change, and acquire dignity thereby."[4] The last sentence of this passage again cautions against hasty judgment on the brittle material of his plots; only in the perspective of a stubborn and apathetic imagination does such disparagement come. Hawthorne multiplies this admonition, not only in his other prefaces, but whenever given the opportunity in his probing sketches on the processes of the creative imagination.[5] From these various comments a tentative principle of Hawthorne's art can be formulated: the literal level of narration in his prose fiction mirrors only the external form of a profounder structure of imaginative truth.

He elaborates this principle of his narrative method still further in a sequence of paradoxes. In one instance he notes that although his "ground-plots" rarely lie "within the widest scope of probability," they nevertheless respect the canon of "homely and natural" truth.[6] In another utterance, coolly indulgent, he acknowledges that he "is apt to invest his plots and characters with the aspect of scenery and people in the clouds, and to steal away the human warmth out of his

conceptions; . . ." yet despite this predilection "a breath of Nature
. . . will find its way into the midst of his fantastic imagery, and
make us feel as if, after all, we were yet within the limits of our
native earth."[7] Ironically sincere, like so many of his other pronouncements on fictional techniques, these two paradoxes clarify his
attitude toward the two aspects of fictional reality: the historical
and the natural. The ground-plot establishes the historical locale
of a narrative: a group of characters moves through a series of
related actions in a specific setting. These movements can be as
incredible as Aylmer's in "The Birthmark" or as convincing as
Donatello's in *The Marble Faun.* Whether or not their environ-
ments and their actions violate the reader's ideas of probability, they
nevertheless conform to the conventions of orthodox fiction: they
enable Hawthorne to give his characters identity in time and space.
On the other hand, "homely and natural" truth, imbued by the
"breath of Nature," offers the assurance that the destinies which they
realize are human. Whether they be a new Adam and Eve or a
Beatrice and Giovanni in different Edens, they react to the caprice
of circumstance like normal human beings. They think and feel in
patterns of response that reflect the nature of total human experience.

As simple as this explanation may be, the fusion of these two
realities in Hawthorne's fiction results in the so-called ambiguity of
his plots and themes. So complex is the intermingling that two
sanctions of interpretation, one from each level of existence, occur
in many of his stories, if not *all* of them. For instance, "The Minister's Black Veil" permits an evaluation of the author's intention in
both the historical and the natural worlds of reality. To insist,
under the first sanction, that Hawthorne unequivocally implies that
Mr. Hooper's sinister black veil concretely embodies the secret sin
in every man's heart negates the former's intense preoccupation with
the responsible moral will. In effect, such an interpretation obscures
the implications of Mr. Hooper's conduct in the province of natural
reality, conduct which exposes his spiritual pride and his prostitution
of his profession. Not only does he ignore the responsibilities of a
minister to teach the efficacy of the good but he also exhibits an

inability to cope with his own predispositions toward evil. Though the veil, on the historical plane of the narrative, functions to enhance the guilt of Mr. Hooper's parishioners, it most cogently comments on their spiritual affinity with him. They betray a moral cowardice identical with his: their fear of fear.) Thus the bizarre line of action in historical time, the influence of an insanely idiosyncratic affectation, inevitably correlates with Hawthorne's subtle indictment of the minister's perversion of the natural basis of human conduct. In other words, the two realities support each other as commentaries upon both historical and natural man: a particular incident in a specific environment serves to illustrate a universally recurrent condition of human nature.

The majority of Hawthorne's tales unfold in these two realities, and the historical projection always defines the literal level of narration. But however unbelievable the historical action may be, its intimations of truth emerge in the realm of human nature where man ceases to be merely a member of society and becomes a part of mankind. Hence any interpretation which arbitrarily delimits one of his tales in time or space violates the intention of his art. This applies even to those works ostensibly adapted from recorded history, as this study will demonstrate.

The two realities of Hawthorne's fictive world present still another problem in technique: the nature of dramatic focus. Since the two phases differ, then each must control a distinguishable province of total human experience. Hawthorne therefore postulates an outer and an inner authority. The historical materialization of his plots defines the external world of man whose elements are all concrete, finite, and identifiable. Law, custom, mores, and convention dictate the norms of the outward behavior of the individual and the group. Social values predominate in this sphere, and morality is a visible, calculable phenomenon. Spiritual life per se is restricted to Hawthorne's other dramatic center: the internal world of man. This invisible and secret existence possesses a special sanctity; it belongs exclusively to the individual, for good or for evil. Value-feelings temper all judgments in this realm. In their moral aspects they embrace the total heritage of man's knowledge of love: of comrade for comrade, of lover for lover, of husband for wife, of wife for husband, of parent for child, of child for parent. By corollary they encompass all the loyalties and responsibilities of each of these vital roles. Conversely, perversions or distortions of these relations of love breed the animosities and hatreds that do violence to natural human sympathies and obligations. As the historical order of reality assimilates the integrating emotions into the structure of its society, so, by the same token, it condemns and punishes the disorganizing expressions of human desire. Hawthorne, in the majority of his short stories and novels, focuses on the inner disorders of feeling which bring his characters into conflict, not only with the external world, but with their own innate predispositions. These intense complications, which defy pragmatic evaluation, send him "burrowing . . . into the depths of our common nature," seeking a psychological solution to the perplexing problem of ethical behavior.[8]

In Hawthorne's vision there is no optimistic belief that man inherently pursues the good life. He is too keen a student of human nature to accept this preposterous assumption. As a consequence, he calmly accepts the existence of evil and argues that it alone confers upon man the mantle of tragic dignity. For despite the fact that the individual will at one time or another find himself in conflict with society and with his own impulses, he must strive for a reconciliation of these opposites, the dissolution of a personal universe of contraries. This mode of salvation is accessible to everyone, but its attainment can come only through the cleansing flames of purgatorial suffering. The agonizing torments of the spirit that Hawthorne minutely details in his works are a fictional projection of this process. Through pain and torment his characters advance toward self-awareness. As this illumination gradually increases, the individual discovers his true self: the whimpering, irresponsible ego that revels in self-deception and treacherous pride. Confronted with this hideous image of the basic imperfection of human nature, he must make a choice. This act of the responsible ethical will involves either a determined and saving effort to wrestle this diabolic force into sacrificing all its desires or a partial or complete surrender to it. If victory comes, the law of morality within prevails. Now the adjustment to the law without follows, for with all spiritual tensions released the individual is transformed into the person that he actually is. This uniqueness, discovered and admitted, condones no selfishness. It adapts itself to the norms of historical existence which arise out of the totality of individual differences. The acceptance of the new role, with all old attitudes, ideas, and beliefs relinquished, betokens a crucial transformation of the spirit: a rebirth.

Even a cursory glance at any of Hawthorne's great novels or short stories reveals that this formula of individual salvation continually operates. Let us briefly examine "The Hollow of the Three Hills," a work generally conceded to be a masterly accomplishment yet never to my knowledge critically justified. In this story Hawthorne reveals an adulteress' encounter with herself in her own conscience — whether in a dream or a nightmare or any other way is immaterial. The evil hag whom she beseeches for knowledge about her kinfolk is herself, and from her she receives the answer. The answer itself is not astonishing: it simply discloses her selfish dereliction of those duties which were hers as wife, parent, and child. In each role she violated her own nature, defiled a holy love with a profane love. Exiled by the society in which she lived to the New World, a setting which she pictures as utterly stagnant and sterile, she literally perishes in the rank quagmire of her own soul.

Akin to her fate is Young Goodman Brown's, whose encounter with his own evilness also occurs in a dream. Unlike the heroine of the other tale, he retreats into an egocentric self-righteousness. What his conscious mind refuses to admit to itself, it projects outward upon members of the community. And thus the future materialization of his destiny is assured. He lives out his life, a sour and sullen man, incapable of love even for his own wife and children. An outcast from humanity in his heart, he is a Wakefield who is charitably granted a place in a home in which he no longer has any meaningful function. Variations on this theme of love in default shape countless other tales, with "Roger Malvin's Burial," in its fantastic atonement, brilliantly anticipating the pronouncements of Jung and Freud upon the vagaries of the psyche, particularly upon the tyrannizing compensations dictated by outraged consciences.

Strangely enough, Hawthorne's "researches in that dusky region"[9] of the inner world compel him to utilize a structural device that savors of a consulting room: the mythic image which tortures the dreams of spiritually distraught patients. Yet in terms of the two realities which govern his conception of narrative method, this detail of technique has a more authoritative precedent, that of organic necessity. Since the meaningful conflicts in his stories are resolved in the consciences of his characters, he requires a dramatic idiom to communicate these experiences. But of greater importance is his need to respect the universal dimensions of this natural order of reality which encompasses the destiny not merely of historical man but of all mankind. In this awareness he perhaps anticipates the pronouncements of Dr. Carl G. Jung, who claims that each mythic image "contain[s] a piece of human psychology and human destiny, a relic of suffering or delight that has happened countless times in our ancestral story."[10] And in dealing, as Hawthorne does, with the movement of thought and emotion across the stage of the theatre of human experience, he perceives in the image a core of revelation that has irresistible appeal to the imagination: its power to excite simultaneously mind and instinct. The choice of the specific mythic form congenial to his investigations invites consideration, for the fates which envelop most of his tragic characters embody suffering in its most destructive and sinister manifestations; in fear and pain and self-loathing, like Dimmesdale in *The Scarlet Letter,* they cower in the darkness of the spirit. And, as T. S. Eliot remarks in *The Cocktail Party,* such a dislocation of the soul

> . . . *can only be hinted at*
> *In myths and images. To speak about it*
> *We talk of darkness, labyrinths, Minotaur terrors.*[11]

The controlling image in Hawthorne's works possesses associations as ancient and compelling as the classical myth of Theseus and Ariadne. Not only does it conform to the requirements of the inner form of his narrative structure but it also meets the crucial requisite of universality, to such a degree that it literally recaptures primitive man's first encounter with fear, the conquest of the sun by darkness. In the recorded history of civilization this dynamic image or its prototype has guided man's understanding of the polarities that characterize the processes of nature and the life of man. The dark principle of the universe, the personification of all the forces hostile to human life, has been known to all civilizations. Ahriman, Tiamat, Set, Vritra, Yin: these are some of the designations of the image which has constantly reminded man that his destiny is molded in strife. Thus, in order to survive, he must conquer, not only the destructive forces of nature, but the undermining powers of negation within himself: hate, anger, fear, and jealousy.

This primordial archetype, as found in the history of Western civilization and particularly in its Christian phase, invests the conflicts in Hawthorne's plots with their moving power. For our sardonic romancer the devil is a myth: Black Man, Satan, Old Nick, Old Scratch, Beelzebub — whatever his disguise at a given moment — he is the reflection of the dark shadows that invade the sunlight of human life. He is the necessary evil in the equation of human destiny. He serves the same kind of role in the myth built around him by Hawthorne as he does in Arnold J. Toynbee's vision of history; he represents the impetus that propels history through its rhythm of rise and fall, of conquest and defeat. The unknown product of civilization, Toynbee asserts, is determined by the effects of an interaction analogous to "some encounter between the Devil and God." This, he goes on to say, "is the plot of the Book of Job and the plot of Goethe's *Faust*"; but "is it, perhaps," he wonderingly inquires, "the plot of life and the plot of history?"[12] Hawthorne leaves no doubt about his answer to the question.

The moral intention of his creative art constitutes his affirmation. Its purpose is to illustrate that the dualism of nature (and of human experience) is the basis of harmony in the universe. Two opposite principles clash. The resolution of the conflict reveals the quality of the secret unity. Only chaos results from a failure to accomplish some form of reconciliation. Hawthorne's attitude on this question explains why, on the one hand, he vehemently denounces the Puritan obsession with evil and, on the other hand, ridicules, as in "The Celestial Railroad," the Unitarian and Transcendental exaggeration of good. Both exist, he insists, to point the way toward harmony. Thus he divorces his creative thought from the rationale of both the subtle theologian and the glib dialectician. A simple mythic formula based on the devil-archetype provides him with the medium of inquiry into the riddle of good and evil. He translates these two forces into the symbolic interaction of God and the devil as they mutually contest the integrity of man's soul. As in the Book of Job, the devil is the adversary, the accuser. He charges that man under conditions of adversity reveals a closer kinship to the evil principle in life than to God. The latter denies this unflattering comment on his own creation. The strife initiated proves that man's millennial quest for truth is neither more nor less than an attempt to discover himself. When an individual learns that he is neither a demon nor a god but rather a meaningful entity unto himself, however imperfect or fallible, then only does he acquire an insight into his own personal role in life. From humility he reaps a harvest of love. He can now accept all the responsibilities of his own unique position in the order of the world.

Hawthorne's insight into the reconciliation of destructive opposites hinges on a still more remarkable conception of the function of the archetypal devil in the moral framework of society. He perceives the apocalyptic value of the image. Whatever the circumstances of its emergence into the mind, its effect is to ease and govern the restlessness of the heart and mind. A monitor of the conscience, it advises the spirit to take inner counsel against evil. The individual must not succumb to the negative influences of the revelation. He must confront the image of the devil where it resides — within himself; for the memory has dredged it up from a conscious association of the past. If he projects the instructive agent outward, insisting that it embodies some evil aspect of the external world, then he prostitutes his ethical will. He refuses to assume the obligations which his own soul thrusts upon him. Recurring instances of this evasion of responsibility lead ultimately to total moral confusion. The lack of inner values urges the supposition that no outer values exist. Thus all evil is vindicated. As the procession of characters in Hawthorne's tales and romances marches into the grinding teeth of conflict, each is forced to make a choice that signifies his particular awareness of a propensity towards evil. Once free will is expressed, the consequences of the act must be borne. Hawthorne provides no easy escapes.

To dramatize the emergence of the devil-image into the mind of a character Hawthorne resorts to the Faustian contract. And as soon as he establishes this relation of ritual with a symbolic image, he lays the substructure of myth which defines the true nature of the universal reality lying beyond the literal narrative level of his fiction. With this added device he indicates when an action parallels a ritual movement — in other words, whenever a character motivation evolves in conjunction with the archetypal ritual. Hawthorne thereby identifies the ensuing response as a symbolic action which, however incredible, denotes the commencement of a moral ordeal. The fable of the basic conflict in Christian mythology authorizes Hawthorne's selection of the archetypal ritual. He reverts to the covenant which fomented strife in the world: Eve's costly bargain with the serpent in the Garden of Eden. This ritual of the selling of the soul to the devil is thus an inevitable addition to Hawthorne's myth.

His preoccupation with this archetypal ritual — perhaps even his dismay at its failure to excite critical appreciation — is elaborated in a semi-autobiographical sketch, "The Devil in Manuscript." In another work, "The Haunted Mind," he concerns himself with its symbolic adaptation to universal human nature. This motif is, of course, not his own invention. In imaginative literature it probably first appeared in the Faust chapbooks during the latter part of the sixteenth century. Christopher Marlowe immediately explored the dramatic possibilities of the theme, and, until the publication of Goethe's

Faust, the play represented the most imaginative treatment of the ritual. Hawthorne, however, owes little or nothing to Marlowe's version of the myth. The romantic proposition that a Faust will sell his soul to the devil only if the reward is surpassing knowledge does violence to Hawthorne's awareness of human nature. The latter's Faust myth is a conception that conforms to all phases of ordinary human experience. Though Goethe concretely influences the shaping of the new myth, Hawthorne also adapts and transforms inspirations from sources as antithetical as the writings of the Puritan divines and the Gothic romancers.

These varied components alone promise a challenging renovation of a familiar mythic ideology. But when he grafts to the trunk of this Faust myth the element of ordeal by sin, he begins to manipulate an idea that colors all cross-cultural hero myths. Whatever the civilization that has spawned these fabulous tales, each recognizes that the hero must pass through a series of trials and tests to prove his physical and spiritual mettle. In short, the twelve labors of Hercules parallel the exploits of countless other adventurers in the voluminous mythologies of past and present cultures. Yet the specific idea of ordeal by sin lifts Hawthorne's Faust myth to a transcendental plane of significance, for in this fashion enlightenment comes to the great religious prophets of mankind: Mohammed, Jesus, Buddha. Thus Hawthorne incorporates in his vision of myth the basic truth of all ages and all times: the vein of iron around which good crystallizes has been tempered in the impurities of evil.

Only by achieving such an imaginative mastery over the role of evil in human existence can Hawthorne control the materials of his fiction. Tragic experience, if it is to have any values of catharsis, must allow the individual to preserve the integrity of his soul even as he plunges into the abyss. Hawthorne's characters, like their author, search their consciences to explain the ambivalence of evil. When they perceive that it lies within as well as without, they attain to the knowledge of a god but not to his ability to circumvent evil. In Hawthorne's own gloomy meditations on his Puritan lineage, the paradox of piety and sin quickens his imagination. When he is able to resolve this paradox through a study of himself and of Puritan history, he is ready to formulate a dynamic Faust myth. As we trace the evolution of this mythic drama throughout this prophetic artist's career, his cumulative fictional achievement synthesizes into an imposing symbolic structure.

CHAPTER II

THE ETHICAL ORIGINS OF HAWTHORNE'S ART

HAWTHORNE'S SPIRITUAL ROOTS are embedded in the Puritan past. Not the pageantry of frontier life, not the social peculiarities of the period, not the recorded achievements of his ancestors primarily absorbed his mind. Although his writings are studded with the striking details of daily existence, his imagination used these concrete facts more to portray mood and to symbolize intellectual preoccupations than to re-create historical events. He was not a writer of history or historical fiction in the ordinary sense. His was not an epic canvas depicting the warfare between the white man and the Indians or the struggle between the colony and its parent empire. The typical materials of realistic fiction, as determined by circumstances of the Puritan environment, seldom enter his tales and romances. He remains indifferent to the commonplace duties, joys, sorrows, and vicissitudes that consitute normal existence. His was a moral, not a graphic, imagination, that betrayed its origin in a haunting feeling of disgrace at the deeds of his forebears, notably John Hathorne, a ruthless witch-hanging judge, and the latter's father, a sadistic Quaker-persecutor. "I, the present writer, as their representative, hereby take shame upon myself for their sakes, . . ."[1] Hawthorne remarked on one occasion.

This sense of guilt, rather than alienating the artist from his inheritance, attracted him to lifelong study of the aberrations of the Puritan soul. With the careful persistence and patience of a scholar he read Puritan history and the books known to have been thumbed by his ancestors. Always he seemed to arrive at the conclusion that a single controlling idea, particularly as symbolized in the satanic character of the Faust story, could explain more clearly than any other conception the essential nature of the New England mind. And in this interpretative framework he also found an approach to the problem of good and evil of his own day and of all time. He had penetrated, he had reason to believe, the mystery of the moral universe.

In the writings of Increase and Cotton Mather, Hawthorne discovered a reliable transcription of the dark ideas that tortured the Puritan conscience. Thereby he derived an insight into the principles of good and evil that molded their convictions. This shade of their thought colored his study of Puritan morality. He perceived that they subscribed to a moral code of exquisite simplicity. The forces of good, all stemming from God, were pitted against the evil hosts of Satan. Though both the devil and God were hidden powers, each pursued his own ends in antagonism to the other, and each used his own instruments. Nevertheless, each had the same territorial design: the conquest of man's spiritual kingdom. Tactically, in the holy war that continually raged, the devil relied upon temptation. Evil in the guise of good was his chief offensive weapon, and his strategic point of attack was man's soul. And since man was a naturally depraved creature, irretrievably tainted by original sin, his soul was in constant jeopardy. Consciously or unconsciously, he could establish a fatal pact with the devil. Therefore the clergymen-generals, all more or less invulnerable in the armor of God's saving grace, functioned as the shock troops of Heaven. Exercising constant vigilance, they with militant determination attacked evil wheresoever it appeared. In the over-all strategy of their campaign, the unrelenting discipline they imposed upon the lay army worked to their advantage. The conditions of the moral life were strictly defined. Any deviation from the accepted norms of behavior was easy to isolate and was quickly punished.

In recording the details of this prodigious struggle between God and Satan, both the Mathers observed that the most shocking example of moral depravity was the individual who, rejecting the eternal bliss of salvation for the transitory pleasures of temporal existence, deliberately sold his soul to the devil. So far as Increase Mather was concerned, in all the literature of heresy Dr. Faustus was the most notorious perpetrator of this type of apostasy. As a consequence he somewhat morbidly assigned to himself the task of compiling a list of the arch-necromancer's sins. Increase Mather's library was designed to expedite this research. He owned the principal works of the sixteenth and seventeenth-century commentators on the renowned magician.[2] He sprinkled the margins of these books with annotations on Faustus or his *famulus,* and these he later wove into *Remarkable Providences* (1684) and *Cases of Conscience Concerning Evil Spirits* (1693). This pedantic preoccupation with a renegade doctor of theology was not without its purpose. In his scholarly investigations of magic under the Christian tradition, Increase had often encountered the fabulous names of Simon Magus, Cyprian of Antioch, Theophilus of Adana, Gerbert, and Zyto,[3] but they had drawn only casual attention, as his marginalia indicate. He could not help noting that the extraordinary list of Faustus' achievements had been arbitrarily borrowed from the historical and legendary accounts of his predecessors. Alert to the dramatic possibilities of his subject, Increase Mather saw, however, that these prepotent wizards, even though they had trafficked with the powers of hell, had never suffered the doom of Faustus, who alone had sold his soul to the devil.

At the time Mather was writing *Remarkable Providences,* even some years before, the English version of the German *Historia von D. Fausten* was a popular and much read book in New England. According to the invoices of a number of Boston booksellers, only the Bible, hymnals, and a few school texts were in greater demand than *The History of the Damnable Life and Deserved Death of Dr. John Faustus.*[4] Mather — there seems little reason to doubt — knew the history well, for he was intimately associated with its importers. Being acquainted with its wide circulation among his parishioners, he was granted countless opportunities to indulge in "Faustsplitting" from the pulpit of the Second North Church in Boston. Though the popularity of the Faust chapbook may have contributed to Mather's

interest in its infamous hero, the quality of his persistent curiosity
was somewhat subtler: it was based on a kind of theological *rapport*.
The damnation of Faustus was in accord with the spiritual politics of
the clergyman's conscience. In terms of Puritan dogma Faustus was
guilty of the sins most abhorrent to the New England mind. Faustus
had sold his soul to the devil; he had denied God, to lose forever the
hope of redemption through salvation.

In relation to Puritan morality, Mather's absorption with Faustus
was easily understandable. The sincerity of his belief in the possibility of personal communion and pact with the devil was unequivocal: "It [witchcraft] had been rejected long agone, by Christian
nations as a thing Superstitious and Diabolical. . . . In some parts
of Germany old *Paganism* Customs are observed more than in other
countries. . . . The Devil is in it all, all Superstition is from him;
and when Secret things, or latent Crimes, are discovered by Superstitious Practices, some Compact and Communion with the Devil is
the Cause of it."[5] His opinions on this subject were normal for the
times. They corresponded in almost every detail to those held in this
country and abroad by educated men. But the feature of Faustus'
apostasy that weighed most heavily on Increase Mather's mind was
the arrogant rejection of salvation. By implication, an epidemic of
similar conduct among the inhabitants of New England might seriously menace the security of colonial Christendom. Nor could it be
forgotten that the dark forests surrounding them were peopled by
Indians who were in league with the satanic legions.

As the Puritan divines were wont to emphasize, salvation through
love of God was the central doctrine of their religion. This clear affirmation of a *summum bonum* that hinged on a supernatural conception of the good made subordination of present to future good a
primary tenet in the conduct of their social and religious life. As
Mather viewed the career of Faustus, he immediately concluded that
the sorcerer had been seduced from God by his very preference for
the illusive pleasures of earthly existence. And to add to this ignominy, Faustus had flouted the omnipotent will of God: he had re-

sorted to magic in an attempt to circumvent the inscrutable workings of the divine mind.

Yet the real import of the Faust story to the moral conscience of Mather is bound up in the theme of temptation. Substituting for his Luciferian Majesty as tempter, Mephistophiles conspires to give satisfaction to every desire that Faustus might have. In distracting the magician's attention from God by the offer of tangible gifts, Mephistophiles blinds him to the pre-eminent good represented in divine grace. The demands of appetite, as Mather and other Puritans generally appraised them, were evil only if they escaped the control of the will. Excess was imprudence. The sin of appetite enslaved the will and the emotions. It obscured God's magnanimous boon of total and lasting happiness in salvation. Mephistophiles, who was aware of this rift in Faustus' moral citadel, was constantly on the alert to assault his senses. He regaled him with the most exotic foods and the most delicate of liquors. When the culprit's despair brought him to the verge of repentance, the malignant fiend conjured the most beautiful women in the world to lure him away from thoughts of God. This latter mode of physical indulgence was indeed accursed. Sexual love, even in wedlock, was conceived as originating in the fall of Adam, and, though a biological function, it was only tolerated as a necessary evil. Intense natural delight was never associated with sacred love. It was to be sublimated in the related virtues of marriage, in parentage, companionship, and mutual fidelity. But these were nothing when judged in the streaming light of divine love. The prior claims that God had on man's love, as Governor Winthrop once stated in a letter to his wife, could not be lightly dismissed: "I am still detayned from thee, but it is by the Lord, who hath a greater interest in me than thy selfe, when his worke is donne he will restore me to thee again to o[u]r mutual comfort."[6] Restraint and moderation, as Mather could see, were anathema to the temperament of Faustus. But still worse, the sexual debauches of Satan's bondsman lacked even the equivocal sanctity of marriage.

The further temptations to which Mephistophiles exposed the

rascally magician had their counterparts in the hierarchy of Puritan moral values. The demonic agent appealed to Faustus' self-interest, supplying him with the magical means to obtain gratuitously any immediate necessity. These easily acquired materialistic gains drove Faustus further beyond the pale of society, and imbued him with a contempt for his orthodox countrymen. He was slowly, thereby, infected by the fatal malady of pride, the secreted poisons of which led to the downfall of his satanic master. Not a whit less corrupting were the favors granted to the friends and acquaintances of the necromancer through the conjurations of Mephistophiles. These indulgences constellated Faustus' doubts in the omnipotence of God. He scoffed at divine providence whose rewards, he thought, were at best questionable.

The most insidious temptation which Mephistophiles devised was also embodied by proscription in the moral code that Mather upheld — the sensuous appeal of the beautiful. Beauty in terms of Puritan ethics was not bad in itself; its evil lay in its ability to obscure the idea of God, from which it drew its delightful harmony.

The truth of this conception was supposedly proved in the religious art of the Catholics, not only in rich vestments and beguiling liturgical music, but also in the lovely statuaries which fostered a devilish iconolatry. The susceptibility of Faustus to beauty was unavoidable; he was, after all, a Renaissance humanist, in the most exalted sense. It was not without reason that the invention of printing was ascribed to him. And when, with the aid of Mephistophiles, he evoked "the famous pearl of Greece," Helen of Troy, he ensnared himself in the atheistic cult of paganism in which beauty was its own excuse for being. The belief in God was here a meaningless abstraction. Thus Mather could concur with the editor of the Faust chapbook in his denunciation of the treachery of the devil: "Wherefore a man may see that the Devil blindeth and enflameth the heart with lust oftentimes, that men fall in love with Harlots, nay even with Furies, which afterward cannot be lightly removed."[7] So beauty seduced the hearts of men away from God. Mather could not see it otherwise.

As horrifying as these lapses from conventional morality were to Mather, they almost lost their importance in the face of the conjurer's unquenchable intellectual curiosity. Not only did Faustus deny the efficacy of knowledge that comes from a love and understanding of God's will, but he flagrantly conspired with the devil to trespass the portals of forbidden knowledge. He aspired for the secrets of heaven and hell; he longed for an insight into the mysteries of the universe that transcended the revelations of Scripture. To fulfill this desire, he considered the loss of his soul but a trivial affair: "Sithence I began to study and speculate the course and order of the Elements, I have not found through the gift that is given me from above, any such learning and wisdom, that can bring me to my desires; and for that I find, that men are unable to instruct me any further in the matter, now have I, Doctor John Faustus, unto the hellish prince of the Orient and his messenger, Mephistophiles, given both body and soul, upon such condition, that they shall learn me, and fulfill my desire in all things."[8] The presumption implicit in this statement by Faustus regarding man's ability to attain self-sufficient knowledge without benefit of heavenly dispensation was construed by the Puritan as a mortal sin. The unduly confident mind which denies the need of faith and humility is a stronghold of overweening pride. To equate the reason of man with the miracle of revelation through faith is inordinately audacious. Man's reliance on the natural powers of his intellect jeopardizes the basis of religion. The perfectionism of the teachings of the church is at once degraded and challenged.[9]

At the outcome every stigma attached to the reputation of Faustus was justified in the eyes of Increase Mather, for the notorious heretic suffered a violent death at the hands of the devil's cohorts. And in further disgrace, the sinner, even though fully conscious of his impiety just before his death, refused to repent. There was hardly a chance that God at the last moment might grant him redeeming grace; but since the ways of God are beyond human comprehension, Faustus might at least have thrown himself upon the mercy of the Lord. The lesson derived from this impious conduct was unmistakable: his spiritual degeneration made genuine remorse impossible.

He had gradually lost his soul as the cleavage between him and his Maker became greater and greater. Obviously Mather could find no better example of moral irresponsibility to give his sermons the quickening leaven of fire and brimstone. The undisciplined life of Faustus formed the perfect antithesis to the moral rigorism which the Puritans advocated and practiced.

The fascination which Faustus exercised upon the imagination of Increase Mather dwindled in the voluminous writings of his son Cotton. The latter did not, by any means, pass silently over the *facile princeps* of magicians. He could not. His library contained almost all the standard works that had Faustus as a subject, along with hundreds of other books on relevant topics of demonology and witchcraft.[10] As a staunch defender of the belief in witchcraft, though of course hostile to its practice, he could not very well close his eyes to its most distinguished practitioner. On one occasion Cotton virtually admitted that Faustus was the devil's most famous convert. Describing the method of argument used by Satan on a victim, he wrote: "The Devil hath constantly come to him by a voice; and he held a constant Discourse with him; and all about Entring into a Contract with him; . . . making many promises to allure him, and telling him many Stories of Dr. Faustus . . . and how he should live deliciously, and have Ease, Comfort, and Money."[11] But Cotton Mather was so intent upon acquiring miscellaneous information that he never took time to synthesize these facts into a coherent interpretation. Faustus was not the symbol of an idea; he was a pedantic fact, one of the blackest items in the record of heretics. Hawthorne, in *Grandfather's Chair,* ridiculed the unassimilated mass of data that Mather carried in his mind. The state of confusion among the Puritan scholar's books was "a visible emblem of the manner in which their contents were crowded into [his] brain." Continuing in the vein of mockery, Hawthorne went on to say of Cotton Mather: "He believed that there were evil spirits all about the world. Doubtless he imagined that they were hidden in the corners and crevices of his library, and that they peeped out from among the leaves of many of his books, as he turned them over, at midnight. He supposed that these unlovely demons were everywhere, in the sunshine as well as in the darkness, and that they were hidden in men's hearts, and stole into their most secret thoughts."[12]

This disparagement of Cotton Mather in no way indicated any dissent by Hawthorne from the major premise of the theologian. If anything, it signified his confidence that he saw the basic pattern of morality that lay hidden behind the Puritan's fuzzy-minded superstitions. Similarly he could detect the logic of Increase Mather's persistent allusions to Faustus' pact with the devil. Stripped of its irrational elements, the scheme of destiny proclaimed by the father and son was a tenable conception of life. Hawthorne discovered that it could function as a symbolic equation of human existence, since it could be balanced by an infinite variety of individual behavior. The compact with the devil, carrying with it a penalty of eternal damnation in hell, elevated man's fate to a level of tragic dignity. Even the most timid of his desires, when they trespassed upon forbidden ground, attained an awful meaning. Whether in thought or act, man figuratively could commit himself to the infernal powers. This method of symbolization imparted a quality of universality to particular manifestations of the individual will. Thus the spiritual dilemma of Young Goodman Brown was not restricted to the environs of a New England village. The problem and its solution belonged to all mankind. Hawthorne's story merely isolated the action in time and space. He did not, however, answer all the questions implicit in Brown's emotional inertia. Hawthorne nevertheless localized the meaning of evil, attributing it less to the negations of the devil than to Brown's disinclination to wrestle with the throttling evil of his own thoughts.

Even in the earliest of his compositions Hawthorne explored the philosophical potential of this central image-group, especially as it fulfilled the function of metaphysical thought without recourse to abstraction. His purpose seemed directed toward a definition of spiritual truth in terms of the influence of good and evil. Thus he depicted the Puritan soul in search of its particular mode of universal morality. To implement his artistic method he took the mythology of superstition, which comprised the world-view of the Mathers, and transformed it into a poetic ideology that gave Puritan experience a new meaning. As he transmuted the conception, he formulated his own Faust myth. This symbolic form, he was quick to realize, was one which generated psycho-philosophical intuitions of tremendous import.

CHAPTER III

HAWTHORNE'S RELATIONS TO THE FAUST
RENAISSANCE IN NEW ENGLAND

HE PUBLICATION of the English translation of Goethe's *Faust* exercised a tremendous influence on intellectual New England in the nineteenth century. No one interested in literature or philosophy escaped its influence, and Hawthorne was no exception. Though the work had been published in 1808, it was not until the 1820's that the masterpiece became generally known to the American public. Two young New Englanders, Edward Everett and George Ticknor, returned in 1817 from an extended *Wanderjahr* in Germany, and in the course of their teaching at Harvard and their numerous writings they attempted to explain the enduring values of *Faust*. In the pages of the *North American Review,* probably the most influential literary magazine of the period, they judicially appraised the structure and the philosophy of the drama. In this activity they were ably abetted by Thomas Carlyle, whose appreciative essays appeared in the *Edinburgh Review,* an imported British periodical of extraordinary popularity. The campaign to spread the merits of Goethe's *Faust* and his other creations developed into a virtual crusade in New England as other critics joined forces with Everett and Ticknor.[1] But not until the complete translation of Part One of *Faust* was available did it really enjoy wide understanding, for previously only its most lauded songs and soliloquies had been translated and published. A. Hayward's prose version (1833) and J. Anster's poetic paraphrase (1835), which were much in demand, helped promote a new appreciation.[2] Interest in the Faust myth itself had been accelerated by the publication in 1826 of Thomas

Roscoe's *The German Novelists*,[3] a collection giving excerpts from
the prose fiction then in favor in Germany. Besides useful critical
and biographical prefaces, it contained tales of *diablerie*, which authors adapted to American settings in the manner of Irving in "The
Devil and Tom Walker."[4] Roscoe's abridgment of the Faust history was preceded by a thorough introduction that placed its hero
in a proper literary and historical perspective, and also provided an
orientation to Goethe's unusual treatment of the magician's life.

But perhaps the outstanding feature of the Faust renaissance in
New England was the increasing attention that was devoted to the
philosophical implications of the Faust myth. Not only Goethe's
drama but also the numerous other works inspired by the myth were
examined for their ideas alone. At a moment when Hawthorne
arrived at a crucial stage in his career of letters, he began to move
in a social circle that included Margaret Fuller, one of the most
dedicated critics of Goethe's *Faust*. About the same time he came
under the influence of George Hillard and Henry Wadsworth
Longfellow, two acute students of German literary thought. It was
shortly after the association with these two scholars that the Faustian definition in his writings deepened, particularly as evinced in
Mosses from an Old Manse; and, as if aware of his debt, Hawthorne
in the introduction to *The Scarlet Letter* confessed that "after growing fastidious by sympathy with the classic refinement of Hillard's
culture" and "after becoming imbued with poetic sentiment at
Longfellow's hearth-stone," he was prompted to "exercise other
faculties of [his] nature. . . ."[5]

No writer in all America went to greater lengths to exalt the
excellence of Goethe's *Faust* than did Margaret Fuller. Not only
did she unceasingly praise the drama in books and magazines, but
she utilized a forceful personality and an eloquent command of
conversation to bring honor to her acknowledged master. As the
first editor of the *Dial,* the mouthpiece of American Transcendentalism, she deserved notice as one of our country's pioneers in philosophical criticism. Her aim in sponsoring the works of a genius like
Goethe was to "give the young . . . a higher standard in thought

and action than would be demanded of them by their own time."[6]
Though she did not succeed in accomplishing this purpose, her
essays in the *Dial* directed the attention of the readers to the deeper
meanings of the Faust myth, especially as it revealed the eighteenth
century's intellectual aspirations "to compass the infinite"; for in
Goethe's *Faust* she saw "shadowed forth . . . the soul of the age,"
which, with all its pretensions, would be in the end "redeemed
by mercy alone." Faust, she claimed, exemplified the spirit of the
age, its discontentment "with the shadowy manifestations of truths
it longed to embrace."[7] Yet Margaret Fuller unveiled more than
the *ethos* of *Faust*. She inadvertently exposed the aspirations of
transcendental New England. This generation of seekers for truth
had rejected the principles of Calvinism for the more liberal plat-
form of Unitarianism, only to discover that no solace could be found
in a spiritual vacuum. Confronted with this harsh fact, they pro-
ceeded to erect their temple of faith on the shaky foundations of a
dubiously interpreted German idealism. Unfortunately, as Hawthorne pointed out, their philosophical edifice rested on a peak in
cloudland, making futile "the search for something real."[8] It was
Hawthorne's deep distrust of the private terminology of the Transcendentalists, who attempted to penetrate the secrets of the moral
universe on the wings of obscure phraseology, that intensified his
preoccupation with mythic imagery. This method of dramatizing
the intellectual pursuit of truth was quickened with metaphorical
thinking that drew its meaning from the spiritual experiences of all
mankind. The ancient myths were not, he once noted, the restricted
imaginative domain of any specific culture; "[They] were the immemorial birthright of mankind." The unique quality of their appeal, he further asserted, made them "the common property of the
world, and of all time. The ancient poets remodelled them at pleasure, and held them plastic in their hands; and why should they not
be plastic in my hands as well?"[9] In realizing that they were "mar-
vellously independent of all temporary modes and circumstances,"[10]
he had unlocked the secret portal to the treasury of mankind's inheritance of ethical symbolism.

In the province of American imaginative fiction Hawthorne was acquainted with Washington Irving's transmutations of Faustian imagery. Having read the *Tales of a Traveller*,[11] he knew "The Devil and Tom Walker," which is usually denominated the "comic New England Faust."[12] The story is set in a gloomy, snake-infested swamp to establish an atmosphere of terror and mystery. Here Tom Walker encounters the devil and sells his soul to acquire the secret location of private gold. After a long career of blackest infamy, Tom is compelled to surrender to his satanic master. He is whisked back to the swamp on a black horse and is never seen again. The comic element in the tale, which derives its spirit from Tom's shrewish wife, actually is a subordinate element in the plot, for Irving permeates the tale with something of the macabre and terrifying mood that characterizes "The Legend of Sleepy Hollow." The black horse is, of course, the animal counterpart of the black dog in the Faust myth. Though the piece lacks intellectual depth, as befits the effects Irving sought, it nevertheless captures the emotional impact of the bargain with the devil.

In Irving's "Wolfert Webber" there is an indication of the influence of Goethe's *Faust*. One of the episodes in the story has analogies with the pranks of Mephistopheles in Auerbach's Cellar.[13] But Irving's notes on a projected play, *El Embozado: The Cloaked Figure*, reveal a more intensive concern with the Faust myth than any other of his published writings. One of his biographers, G. S. Hellman, cites the unfinished work as "an incomplete Faust drama." The plot, designed to revolve around the dual nature of man, was to embrace acts of crime and seduction from which the hero is finally saved through the intervention of the moral side of his personality. While Hellman registers doubt that Irving was capable of the intellectual and philosophical flights required in his plot,[14] the abortive Faust production nevertheless serves to bring home the stimulating nature of Faustian imagery in regard to salvation through the ordeal of sin. Like many another creative genius who had pondered this symbolism, he felt the urge to pour his own meditations on good and evil into the mold of this ancient prototype.

To an even greater degree, Hawthorne's Bowdoin classmate Long-fellow was an imaginative thrall to the Faustian archetype through the many years of his career as a teacher and a writer. Having come to understand German culture during his tours abroad, he was equipped to interpret the German literature that he so passionately loved. His lectures at Harvard on Goethe's *Faust* represented the peak of sound scholarship and research, and over a long period of time he had no peer in the historical knowledge of the Faust myth. Longfellow's teaching copy of Part One of *Faust* lends authority to this statement. The notes scrawled on the blank leaves cover most of the subjects that would be treated in a modern discussion. He traced the tradition of the motivating impulse of the myth, the sell-ing of the soul to the devil, through folklore and mythology. He recapitulated the available facts that support the existence of a historical Faust. He was familiar with the first Faust chapbook, as he was with the adaptations of the theme in drama and the puppet shows. In marginalia he jotted many illuminating parallels to single passages — from the Sanskrit, the Bible, Old English, Rabbinical literature, the Edda, the legends of the saints, and poetry in several languages. Conversant with the magic ritual employed to conjure the devil, he described the well-known Faust "Pentagram" as a sign used all over Asia for a charm against witchcraft. Exploring the belief in Christian thought, he exhibited an acute insight into the development and metamorphosis of ancient superstitions, especially as they impinged upon religious beliefs. In short, Longfellow's copy of *Faust* is an astounding compendium of Faustian imagery.[15] Yet his imagination never bridged the final gap to complete understand-ing of the materials which he had accumulated. In the unbroken recurrence of this symbolism in ritual practice he ignored its uses as an educative medium that taught endless generations of man to profit from their experiences with evil. All in all, however, Long-fellow was the most thorough Faust scholar of the day.[16]

This knowledge colored the poet's own creative writings. Goethe's *Faust* in particular served as the source of countless allusions in his poetry and prose. But on occasions he adapted a motif out of the myth to his own purposes. The chapter on the homunculus in *Hyperion,* though it appears in Goethe's work, originally found expression in the Wagner Book of the Faust cycle. Even in Longfellow's project for a "New England Faust" that would follow "the old tradition of selling one's soul to the devil,"[17] he relied upon the trappings of his scholarship; for "The Golden Legend," the abortive result, was a derivative Faustian drama. His devotion to Goethe also took another form. In 1837 at Harvard he inaugurated a series of lectures on the German poet. And for months before the session of college opened, he prepared his lecture notes, but not without seeking encouragement for the method of presentation in letters to interested persons.[18] This evident search for a congenial and intimate associate with whom to share the excitement of his investigations and studies was resolved by a coincidence. Just six months before the school year began, he received a letter from an old Bowdoin classmate — Nathaniel Hawthorne.

Promoting his *Twice-Told Tales,* Hawthorne requested that Longfellow accept a copy of the recently published volume, and at the same time praised the latter's *Outre-Mer.*[19] Longfellow answered the letter very cordially, and then capped his expressed appreciation for the work with a highly laudatory review in the *North American Review.* By the end of the fall term the friendship between the two men was strongly knitted. Not only did they frequently walk and dine together, but their literary intimacy was highly confidential. Longfellow had apparently found a sensitive confidant in his major field of endeavor. Hawthorne's letter of March 21, 1838, to his friend leaves no doubt about this point:

I was sorry that you did not come to dinner on Sunday, for I wanted to have a talk with you about the book of Fairy Tales which you spoke of. I think it a good idea, and am well inclined to do my part toward the execution of it. . . . Not but what I am terribly harassed with magazine scribbling, and, moreover, have had overtures from two different quarters to perpetrate children's histories and other such iniquities. But it seems to me that your book will be more credible, and perhaps quite as profitable. Possibly we may make a great hit, and entirely revolutionize the whole system of juvenile literature.[20]

On occasions Longfellow visited Hawthorne's home in the eccentric atmosphere of Herbert Street in Salem. To be sure, they spent little time there; rather, they adjourned to the Coffee House in town and there, as Longfellow noted in his journal — "Passed the afternoon with him, discussing literary matters. [He is] a man of genius and a fine imagination."[21] The frequency of these meetings between the two writers is impossible to estimate, but during the year 1838, whenever they did get together, the association lasted several hours. In a letter to George W. Greene, Longfellow confided: "I shall see Hawthorne tomorrow. He lives in Salem, and we are to meet and sup together tomorrow evening at the Tremont House. . . . He is a strange owl; a very peculiar individual, with a dash of originality about him that is very pleasant to behold."[22] It is significant that at this time Longfellow was writing *Hyperion,* a work in which he devoted a whole chapter to Goethe's genius, with copious citations from Parts One and Two of *Faust.* Moreover, in his letters and journals, he constantly alluded to preparations for the Faust lectures.[23]

In 1839 Hawthorne moved from Salem to Boston in order to take a job as weigher in the Boston Custom House. The appointment had been secured through the united efforts of Hawthorne's future sister-in-law Elizabeth Peabody and George Bancroft. When Hawthorne learned of his good fortune, he immediately dispatched the news to Longfellow: "I shall remove to Boston in the course of a fortnight, and, most sincerely, I do not know that I have any pleasanter anticipation than that of frequently meeting you."[24] It seems highly probable that it was as a result of this letter that Hawthorne came to occupy a room in the residence of George Hillard in Boston. Hillard belonged to the brilliant coterie of Cambridge literary men which included Longfellow, Charles Sumner, and Edward Felton. Later Hillard was to become one of Hawthorne's most faithful and serviceable friends. He introduced him to the publishers Ticknor and Fields; he collected a substantial purse to carry Hawthorne through a period of financial crisis; and he was the lawyer in the Brook Farm

litigation against George Ripley, as well as the executor of Hawthorne's estate after the latter's death.

Hawthorne's proximity to Harvard gave added impetus to his
friendship with Longfellow, and threw him into the company of a
group of scholars who were profoundly interested in things German.[25] An entry in Longfellow's journal depicts the mode of social
intercourse: "Hawthorne came to pass the evening. We had a long
conversation on literature. He means to write a child's book. I told
him of my ballad, and that I meant to have it printed on a sheet
with a picture on top, like other ballads. He is delighted with the
idea; and says he will distribute them to every skipper of every craft
he boards in his custom-house duties, so as to hear their criticisms.
Hillard and Felton came late, and we had a pleasant supper."[26]

What thoughts Hawthorne carried away from such rich evenings,
it is impossible to determine. But surely Goethe and his *Faust* must
often have been a topic of conversation. Longfellow's current Faust
writings and lectures, so much on his mind, must have been thor-
oughly aired over the after-dinner port. This intimacy probably
broadened Hawthorne's knowledge of the Faust myth in general,
and gave him new insights into the meaning of Goethe's *Faust*. He
was already familiar with the external mechanics of Faustian imagery, his readings in the Mathers, in the current literature of witchcraft, and in the contemporary periodicals having filled out this
background. As his circle of friends widened through his relations
with Longfellow and through his engagement to Sophia Peabody,
he was exposed, more and more, to German variations of the subject.

Yet even in the solitary years that he spent in Salem, perfecting
his art and producing a miscellaneous group of tales, his conception
of the devil-image and the ritual act of selling the soul to the devil
had developed beyond a theological phase. Always concerned with
the function of evil in human behavior, he was too meditative and
critical, if not too skeptical, to accept literally the value of the symbols in Calvinistic religion. His youthful exposure to the zealous
chest-pounding of the Mathers first encouraged him to search for
"the empirical truth behind Calvinistic symbols,"[27] but with the

aim of reducing these findings to their spiritual essence. Hence, at
the outset of his writing career, within the framework of many of
his short stories, he dallied with a Faustian thesis, shaping it to fit his
speculations on human destiny. Long before contemporary critics
turned their attentions to the Pelagian implications of *Faust,* Hawthorne had directed his mind along the same paths of thought as
Goethe. He facetiously described this compulsion in "Sights from
a Steeple" in 1831: "O that the Limping Devil of Le Sage would
perch beside me here, and extend his wand over this contiguity of
roofs, uncover every chamber, and make me familiar with their
inhabitants! The most desirable mode of existence might be that of
a spiritualized Paul Pry, hovering invisible round man and woman,
witnessing their deeds, searching into their hearts, borrowing bright-
ness from their felicity and shade from their sorrow, and retaining
no emotion peculiar to himself."[28] Here perhaps was the dawning
recognition that the devil, despite his putative evil, could serve man
profitably.

The comparative solitude in which he lived between 1825 and
1837 contracted the range of what might be termed Faustian definition. But the materials which he molded into his tales did not
derive from personal experience; they were culled out of his voluminous reading. Though he perhaps carried the practice to extremes,
he somehow managed to maintain a singular detachment which
enabled him to penetrate to the basic truths of the books he read.
This dispassionate intellectual attitude, a composite of philosophical
and psychological awareness, permitted him to transcend his raw
inspiration — to face a grim and challenging reality. Thus his
friendship with Longfellow, his participation, however reluctant, in
the affairs of the Peabody circle, and his commonplace but exciting
duties in the Boston Custom House were to season his observations
on life with a new pungency. This change is reflected in the differ-
ence between *Twice-Told Tales* and *Mosses from an Old Manse,*
if we keep in mind the legitimate chronology of the tales. If the
deepening tide of his thinking, the satire and irony which propel his
pen, and the acerbity of perception seem irreconcilable with the

happiest days of his marriage to Sophia Peabody, the answer is to be found in Hawthorne's concern with the problem of good and evil posed most dramatically in Goethe's *Faust*, a challenge which forced him to minimize his personal happiness. His thoughts, strengthened by contact with the world of men and affairs and sharpened by the fulfillment of his sexual passions, no longer had "the pale tint of flowers that blossomed in too retired a shade. . . ."[29]

Even before Herman Melville was on intimate terms with Hawthorne, he perceived the unusual quality of *Mosses from an Old Manse*. Well aware of the darkness which clouded his own soul, he penetrated the gloom that shadowed the most joyful of Hawthorne's tales. He saw that the New Englander's focus on evil was geared to some higher purpose:

For, in certain moods, no man can weigh this world without throwing in some thing, somehow like Original Sin, to strike the uneven balance. At all events, perhaps no writer has ever wielded this terrific thought with greater terror than this same harmless Hawthorne. Still more: this black conceit pervades him through and through. You may be witched by his sunlight — transported by the bright gildings in the skies he builds over you; but there is the blackness of the darkness beyond; and even his bright gildings but fringe and play upon the edges of thunder-clouds. In one word, the world is mistaken in this Nathaniel Hawthorne. He himself must often have smiled at its absurd misconception of him. He is immeasurably deeper than the plummet of the mere critic. For it is not the brain that can test such a man; it is only the heart. You cannot come to know greatness by inspecting it; there is no glimpse to be caught of it, except by intuition; you need not ring it, you but touch it, and you find it is gold.[30]

These observations imply Melville's spiritual and imaginative kinship with Hawthorne. Without having met the latter, he nevertheless sensed his creative mission. In effect, he believed that Hawthorne's apparent preoccupation with the darkest aspects of Calvinistic dogma disclosed not especially a theological bias but rather a consciousness of man's necessity to somehow overpower his predispositions toward evil. There was no desire on Hawthorne's part to remold life nearer to the heart's desire. It was man's duty to resolve his destiny in this vale of tears: to assume responsibility for his personal moral defections. His tales in the *Mosses* record individual instances of the struggle to make this adjustment.

After Hawthorne terminated his employment in the Boston Custom House, he returned to his home in Salem, in January, 1846. At this time the little community was enveloped, like so many others in the vicinity of Boston, in the electric atmosphere of Transcendentalism. Sophia Peabody was a rapt admirer of Emerson. Her sister and mother operated a bookstore which was the center of the new intellectual movement. Here was sold the literature of its disciples, not only the pamphlets of its American proponents, but also the writings of the men who had enormously affected the development of the spiritual values espoused by the group. Coleridge and Kant were two of the prominent names to be glimpsed on the well-stocked shelves. And here it was that Margaret Fuller initiated her conversations on German literature and other topics. These monologues were admirable stimulants to the sale of the unusual books and journals which the Peabodys dispensed: George Ripley's translations of modern German literature, Carlyle's works, and the English periodicals that specialized in translations of continental writers.[31] Without doubt Margaret Fuller's *Eckermann's Conversations with Goethe* was strategically exhibited in the shop, along with some of the translations of Goethe's *Faust* that were current. In effect, Hawthorne's Salem environment provided a further stimulant to the interests that he had cultivated in his association with the Cambridge intelligentsia.

Thus the design of the Salem artist's life at this time was inseparable from the New England cult of Goethe and *Faust*. Whether he lived in Boston, in Salem, or on Brook Farm, he encountered "few educated people who could not talk with glib delight about German literature."[32] Even native American drama had taken on the impress of the Faust myth through the influence of Byron and Goethe.[33] And in the genre of the Gothic romance, the art form

which most appealed to Hawthorne, Faustian symbolism was a
standard ingredient. But whereas most of Hawthorne's predecessors,
like his own contemporary Poe, used the conventions to activate an
outer world of false supernaturalism, he instead relied upon diabolic
imagery to animate the inner sphere of a psychological and philosophical reality. In this way a static symbolism of terror was transformed into an ethical instrument. It became the symbolic center
of the moral world which Hawthorne surveyed with a curious eye.

CHAPTER IV

FAUSTIAN SYMBOLISM IN THE GOTHIC ROMANCE

AWTHORNE'S RENOVATION of the Gothic tale, which introduced a new conception of the dynamic quality of symbols, perhaps explains his reluctance to change his narrative methods. In English and American fiction he had ample proof that new developments were outmoding the genre of suspense and terror. Scott and Cooper had established the popularity of the historical romance; Dickens and others had pioneered the humanitarian narrative. The sentimental novel, which Richardson had skillfully fashioned in the eighteenth century, still had its following. Yet Hawthorne persisted in retaining nearly all the Gothic machinery of Walpole, Radcliffe, Lewis, Maturin, and Godwin. Magical practices, mysterious portraits, enchanted mirrors, transformations, elixirs of life, haunted houses: these are the devices used at one time or another by Hawthorne. But in their manipulation he departed from the customary procedures of his predecessors. He converted these Gothic phenomena into symbols. Not the excitement of morbid or superstitious fears was his purpose; he sought to interpret the wonder and mystery of life, dissociated from a mere appeal to sensibility. In the realm of magic, the evocation of the devil is emblematic of illicit inquiry into the reason for man's being. The mysterious portraits in *The House of the Seven Gables* or "Edward Randolph's Portrait" are less instruments of horror than personifications of the evil that controls the moral will of humanity. The enchanted mirror of Cornelius Agrippa in "A Virtuoso's Collection" holds the answer to the problem of human existence in "Monsieur du Miroir." The transformation of Hester into a genuinely social-minded creature and of Chillingworth from a respectable scholar into a demon represents two contrasting phases of ethical development, growth into or isolation from the common world, as dictated by experience with evil. The elixir of life in *Septimius Felton* and "Dr. Heidegger's Experiment" poses an identical problem of individual isolation from society, which can be solved in one of two ways according to an acceptance or rejection of one's personal inclination toward evil. The haunted house, most aptly symbolized in *The House of the Seven Gables,* stands as a monument to the iniquities of selfish ambition and dynastic pride. These operative symbols possess two qualities that distinguish them from their prototypes in the Gothic romance. First, each symbol generates a body of ideas pertaining to human destiny; the original static token is thus endowed with a dynamic principle. Second, the symbols seldom function as insulated units of meaning; most often they are corollary manifestations of the major thematic symbol, the mythic devil and the mythic ritual of selling the soul to the devil. Therefore the Faustian implications of Hawthorne's thought are always present.

It is no coincidence, then, that Hawthorne's writings have numerous parallels in the Gothic romance. However, the fact that these analogies most frequently occur in works that employ conventions of the Faust myth seems to indicate a definite bias in his choice of materials. William Beckford's *Vathek* (1786) illustrates the point. This novel, an excursion into Oriental Gothic, utilizes the common motivations of the Faust myth. Once the romance is stripped of its exotic veneer, three basic elements of the myth are revealed: the desire for knowledge beyond the limits of human power; the dabbling in magic; and the pact with a satanic agent. Beckford adopted this plot at a time in the eighteenth century when the Faust story was the topic of innumerable farces, harlequinades, and puppet shows.[1] His treatment emphasizes the most sordid character of the myth. The pact with the devil is based on the usual exchange of eternal bliss for temporal pleasures, and Beckford's hero takes every advantage of the license he receives to satisfy his criminal desires,

mayhem and murder becoming the convenient method of intimidation. This sensational context embraces the general substance of
the plot. But only one aspect of *Vathek* apparently attracted Hawthorne — the symbolic content in the last chapter of the novel.
Vathek and his paramour, who are lured into an Oriental purga-
tory, view the incessant parade of a multitude of the devil's votaries,
"who severally [keep] their right hands on their hearts." By this
fixed gesture they attempt to hide their hearts, which are enveloped
in flames. The two lovers are doomed to suffer this horrible and
eternal fate in punishment of "unrestrained passions and atrocious
actions. Such is . . . the chastisement of blind ambition, that would
transgress those bounds which the Creator hath prescribed to human
Knowledge; and, by aiming at discoveries reserved for pure Intelligence, acquire that infatuated pride, which perceives not that the
condition appointed to man is to be ignorant and humble."[2] Hawthorne adapts two details of Beckford's symbolism in *The Scarlet
Letter*. The ignited heart becomes symbolic of the flames of evil
which gradually consume the vital organ of goodness in Chillingworth's breast. Dimmesdale acquires the gesture of the right hand
over the heart, for there again was the seat of malevolent passion
that goaded him into the sins of the flesh. The speculative considerations which these two symbols provoke in Hawthorne's romance
give them a highly original function that elevates their use above
the merely spectacular purpose of Beckford's *Vathek*.

Matthew Gregory Lewis' *The Monk* (1795), which draws its
motive power from the Faust theme, was probably the source of
Hawthorne's "monk-temptress"[3] theme in *The Scarlet Letter*. The
idea of the sexual temptation of saints is of course as old as the
Christian tradition or, more accurately, human civilization. In its
most familiar form it is embodied in many tales of *The Golden
Legend* and the *Gesta Romanorum*. In the Faust myth this form of
temptation has its own peculiar trademark. Primarily it is a seduction designed to expedite a compact with the devil. However, at
times the stratagem is applied to deter repentance. Lewis relies upon
these two variations in *The Monk*. Ambrosio, a monk much ad-

mired for his austere holiness, is guilty of spiritual pride, having
never been subjected to the allurements of evil. Satan therefore
sends a beautiful girl disguised as a novice to tempt Ambrosio.
Having once given expression to a hitherto sublimated sexual drive,
the monk cannot control himself. The temptress goads him on to
rape and murder. But whenever the possibility of repentance arises,
she contrives still more irresistible pleasures. At length Ambrosio,
to escape the torments of inquisition, is compelled to sign a contract
with the demon, but he only suffers a violent death at the hands of
his mocking savior.

Hawthorne skillfully adapts these motivations in the relationship
of Hester Prynne and Dimmesdale. Dimmesdale is portrayed as a
man of strong animal passions. Like Ambrosio, he is also famous
for his abnormal piety. In a moment of passion Hester and Dimmesdale yield to the strong sensual forces in their natures. The minister
resists further temptations after Hester is disgraced by an illegitimate child, and he attempts to compensate for his sin by engaging
in the most rigorous penance. He does not, however, truly repent.
As a consequence, he has no reason to expect salvation according to
Calvinistic dogma. Yet he is not actually committed to the cause of
the devil, for he is remorseful, though without conviction of having
done wrong. Grace is still possible. Hester, unlike her lover, wishes
to perpetuate the sin. She wants earthly happiness with the minister.
Indifferent to the hope of salvation, she persuades Dimmesdale to
seek a new life for them in another country. Dimmesdale agrees to
her plan only after Hester destroys all his will power. He loses his
entire moral perspective when, meeting Hester in the forest, he is
again exposed to her intense sexual attraction. She deliberately
heightens her charm by casting away her scarlet letter and by loos-
ing her lovely dark hair. After he leaves Hester, the minister knows
that he has been duped into making a covenant with the devil. If
he leaves the locale of his sin, he cannot expect mercy from God,
for if he is to repent it must be before the community. Here Hawthorne transforms his source beyond immediate recognition; yet it
retains the distinctive spirit of the similar situation in *The Monk*.

The binding pact with the Infernus, initiated with a Faustian twist in Lewis' work, was in accord with the intricacies of Hawthorne's art. The latter could not overlook its dramatic potential.

In William Godwin's *Caleb Williams* (1794) and *St. Leon* (1799) Hawthorne found Gothic machinery devoted to the end of moral preachments. While Godwin wrote his novels to propagate his own sociological and philosophical ideas, he resorted to the formula of the Gothic romance as a means of vivifying his abstract theses. His aim in *Caleb Williams* is to amplify the vicious extremes of social tyranny. Though he utilizes Gothic devices, he strives less to create an atmosphere of supernatural tension than to offer a psychological explanation for the behavior of his chief character. Caleb Williams is depicted in a flight to escape the revengeful plans of his master, a man exercising extraordinary influence over the conduct of the political officials. No matter where Caleb goes, he is subject to the intimidation of his employer's agents. Never permitted a moment's peace and forced to change his residence almost daily, Caleb is overwhelmed by apprehensions that assume the character of madness. Curiously enough, all the trouble which overtakes him has its derivation in overmastering curiosity, one of the facets of the Faustian world-view. As the inclination is examined in the novel, the associations flowing therefrom are allied to a bargain with the devil: "To gratify a foolishly inquisitive humor you have sold yourself."[4] Inordinate curiosity therefore becomes a kind of psychological symbol of the kind of behavior that is incited by the enemy of mankind. Variants of this idea appear in Hawthorne's works. Ethan Brand's search for the unpardonable sin is an example of the form the habit might take.

Godwin's *St. Leon,* the hero of which learns the secret of the elixir of life through contact with a mysterious Italian, is intended to show the difficulty entailed in any attempt to improve the lot of mankind. However, as the plot unfolds, St. Leon's supernaturally prolonged existence is a vain possession. The knowledge which he accumulates isolates him from mankind. His eternal youth, devoid of all natural warmth, alienates him from the ordinary desires of the human heart. Though his endowment represents a vast fund of possible good, his inability to establish emotional rapport with his fellow creatures neutralizes his stupendous powers. Thus Godwin delineates one of the philosophical problems implicit in the Faust myth: illicit knowledge gives ambition a scope that blinds the individual to the common basis of human happiness. Hawthorne's Septimius Felton, like all Fausts, is entangled in this same dilemma. The elixir of life, which was to be the touchstone of his achievements, corrupts his ideals. His ambitions lose connection with the aspirations of the normal soul.

Charles Robert Maturin's *Melmoth the Wanderer* (1820) has been designated one of the four masterpieces of Gothic romance, the others being *The Mysteries of Udolpho, The Italian,* and *The Monk.*[5] The superb imaginative conception which gave birth to the novel was perhaps the guarantee of its exciting qualities, for it was the first of the English Gothic productions to be influenced directly by Goethe's finally rendered version of Part One of *Faust.* Maturin took the Fausts of myth and of Goethe and cunningly blended them with the mocking spirit of Mephistopheles. This ingenious synthesis finds a notable parallel in Hawthorne's *The Scarlet Letter.* Chillingworth is a unique fusion of the typical Faustian hero and the Mephistophelian tempter of the Puritan tradition.

An entry in Hawthorne's journal indicates that another element of Maturin's characterization of John Melmoth drew his attention. Hawthorne entered the following idea for a story in 1835: "In a dream to wander to some place where may be heard the complaints of all the miserable on earth."[6] This germinal situation is the basis of Maturin's story. He contrives a pact for Melmoth that involves intercourse among people exposed to the most unutterable miseries. Melmoth, "whose intellectual vessel was too great for the narrow seas where it was coasting,"[7] bargains his soul away for the privilege of living one hundred and fifty years. The devil, with characteristic irony, assures Melmoth that he can nullify the contract if he can find anyone who is willing to forgo divine immortality in exchange for the powers of magic in Melmoth's possession. Melmoth soon discovers that the boon of extended existence is only the root of dark and endless despair. Consequently, in the manner of the Wandering Jew, Melmoth roams restlessly over the face of the earth in search of the person who to gain surcease from sorrow will sell his soul. Wherever there is a man in desperate straits, there Melmoth appears to argue his case. Though he presents his evidence with the skill and conviction of a Mephistopheles, he does not achieve his goal. The most wretched people are still fortified by their certainty of ultimate salvation. However much Melmoth mocks their condition or ridicules their beliefs, they are not shaken from their stand. Subsequently he meets a horrible fate at the hands of Lucifer: he is thrown to his death from the dizzy heights of a towering pinnacle. This catastrophe, which also has its analogy in *The Monk,* contributes several details of Butler's death in Hawthorne's *Fanshawe.* Maturin's description of the incident provides the reason: "He fell, and falling grasped aught that might save him. His fall seemed perpendicular — there was nought to save him — the rock was smooth as ice — the ocean of fire broke at his feet . . . he fell — he blazed — he shrieked."[8] The violent end met by these two disciples of the devil is firmly embedded, not only in the antecedents of the Faust myth, but also in the chapbook histories of the archrogue. As evidenced by Hawthorne's apparent borrowings from *Melmoth the Wanderer,* his imagination reveled in Maturin's original improvisations on Goethe's *Faust.* The tragic variations which Maturin introduced through his modification of the devil's contract may have influenced Hawthorne's numerous interpolations in the same area of thought.

In George William MacArthur Reynolds' *Faust,* also, the treatment of the myth is characterized by imaginative fertility. The hero of the story, Faust, sells his soul to the devil so that he can attain "power, vengeance, and triumph."[9] Faust is tricked into the contract by the demon who, by conjuring up the young man's sweetheart in a magic mirror, is able to convince Faust that she is false. The revenge which he is promised outweighs the value of his soul. Another of Reynolds' details is still more ingenious. Taking the twenty-four years of the pact's duration, which is a convention of the chapbook and of Marlowe's *Faustus*, Reynolds has Satan grant Faust an equivalent period of infernal freedom only on condition that the latter's first-born child be at the service of the diabolic powers. Faust, however, manages to free his son from demonic control. The boy is miraculously restored to his normal place in the world by the intervention of a zealous Christian who climbs Mount Ararat to touch Noah's ark. This act of preternatural piety, accomplished against the rigorous opposition and temptations of the devil, effects the desired change. It is interesting to note that the motive of revenge leads Chillingworth into a pact with the devil in *The Scarlet Letter*. And in the same novel Pearl's transformation occurs only after Dimmesdale conquers his tempter and makes a public confession of his sin of fornication. These rather impressive parallels point to Reynolds' *Faust* as one of the many sources of *The Scarlet Letter*. In the case of the transformation Hawthorne discovered a symbol in *Faust* that could explain Pearl's conversion from a child of Satan into one of God's creatures. Having been born in sin, Pearl could assume her legitimate position in life only through the identification of her father. Dimmesdale's rehearsal of his moral crime gave her status in the human community.

Perhaps the most fantastically original tale in the Faust tradition in the early nineteenth century was written in Germany. E. T. A. Hoffmann's *The Devil's Elixir*, which is motivated by a "monk-temptress" theme similar to that of *The Monk*, offers an admirable adaptation of the elixir-of-life motif. Hoffmann changes this device of Gothic machinery into a symbol of psychological reference, and uses it to illuminate the behavior of his chief character, the monk Medardus. The monk, who secretly avails himself of a devil-distilled elixir, a relic of the monastery, believes that the diabolic potion is responsible for his fame as a preacher. Although the elixir is exhibited to deceive gullible pilgrims, Medardus thinks that by quaffing the drink he has sold his soul to the devil. This delusion is the logical outcome of his formalized religious training, which explains unusual happenings in terms of either God or Satan. So morbidly self-conscious does he become about this and other sins that he continually seeks to probe into the secret lives of other men, a propensity for which he is condemned: ". . . thou venturest, like the most pure — nay, like the Divinity whom thou blasphemest, to look into the secrets of my bosom."[10] And here there is a disturbing prototype of Dimmesdale's denouncement of Chillingworth's identical presumption in *The Scarlet Letter:* "That old man's revenge has been blacker than my sin. He has violated, in cold blood, the sanctity of a human heart."[11] And not unlike Chillingworth's insidious tormenting of the Puritan divine, Medardus, "mocking at all conventional limitations,"[12] desires "to exert empire over the insipid beings . . ."[13] whom he controls by virtue of friendship and of ecclesiastical position. But base deception and murder become the instruments of his ambition. Yet even though his crimes increase in violence and cruelty, he cannot suppress his moral education, which continually tortures his conscience in much the same manner that early religious conditioning contributes to Chillingworth's gloomy fatalism.

To banish remorse, Medardus engages in still further abuses of conventional morality. Simultaneously his physical appearance begins to change: "It seems, as if the mind, accommodating itself to the ruling principle, worked outwardly in such a manner, that even the bodily form becomes plastic, moulding itself in turn according to that plan which the higher powers of volition had conceived and laid down."[14] And to explain Chillingworth's physical deterioration Hawthorne invokes a generalization equivalent to Hoffmann's: "In a word, old Roger Chillingworth was a striking evidence of man's faculty of transforming himself into a devil, if he will only, for a reasonable space of time, undertake a devil's office. This unhappy person had effected such a transformation, by devoting himself, for seven years, to the constant analysis of a heart full of torture, and deriving his enjoyment thence, and adding fuel to those fiery tortures which he analyzed and gloated over."[15] Only in the fidelity to the pervasive devil-symbol does this passage differ from the one above.

The characterizations of the two villains continue to evolve in a concurrent pattern. As time passes, the struggle in Medardus' conscience between good and evil drives him to the brink of insanity. The more his instincts warn him that he must pay the devil his due, the closer becomes his affinity to sin. He need only glance at a stranger, and he is able to estimate the evil in that person's heart. This terrible power of insight into sin is the sign of a completely disorganized mind: "It is a peculiar attribute of madmen that they can look more deeply into the hearts of those by whom they are surrounded."[16] So firmly does the conviction of unregenerate evil possess his mind that he is subject to hallucinations. He thinks himself haunted by a double, who speaks in the tones of the devil himself; his distorted imagination continually recreates the conversation of the inner Satan: "Seest thou, now, Medardus, it began (the internal voice), how thou triumph'st over all the conditional laws and limitations of this life — how Destiny now submits herself to thy will, and only knots more firmly the threads which thou thyself hadst spun."[17]

Thus Hoffmann, by converting two elements of the Faust story, the elixir of life and the pact with the devil, into psychological symbols, achieves artistic freedom to probe into an unexplored dimension of human ambition: the desire to dominate the minds of other men. The method is rendered especially effective by the dramatic contrast which Hoffmann establishes between moral and intellectual volition. The subtle kinship between man's spiritual and physical natures enables him to create another zone of strife and contrast. This innovation in Gothic technique, the symbolization of the activities in the theatre of the conscience, comprises Hoffmann's contribution to the literature of suspense and terror.

Hawthorne further developed this literary method. He unobtrusively merged the material and the immaterial worlds to enhance complete poetic acceptance. In *The Scarlet Letter* both Hester and Dimmesdale are haunted by the demon of their conscience, who mocks their feeble resistance to sin. Medardus' physical and spiritual devolution, as has been pointed out, anticipates that of Chillingworth, even to the detail of his aspiring for spiritual domination over another person. But whereas Hoffmann at times inadequately conveys his impressions through the use of symbols, since he but rarely embellishes the symbol with additional commentary, Hawthorne amplifies the symbol, in both its philosophical and psychological implications. The commission of evil for Hawthorne was no isolated event in a circumscribed psychological world; in the scheme of universal morality evil challenged definition. No theological dogma gave it meaning; no convention evaluated it; on the contrary, its shape was hidden in the chaos of ideals that motivate imperfect man. Hawthorne probed this problem in all of his novels, and devoted most of his tales to a search for a valid statement of its function in human existence.

Though Honoré de Balzac can hardly be designated a Gothic romancer, in several of the *Philosophic Studies* he focused his sharp French intelligence upon a number of supernatural motifs that fall into the framework of the Faust myth and into designs of Hawthorne's writings. As the classifying title of these stories indicates, he considered these functional ideas, apart from mere narrative concern, in their proper role as cultural values. As such, in his wide and sweeping vision, they had to be appraised in terms of their relation to the vital forces of thought that direct the course of human society. Subsuming all his cogitations on the subject of illicit knowledge, as defined by Faustian magic, was the belief that religion, whether a great mythology of the conscience or an expression of divine will, exercised the only efficacious control over man's essentially unintegrated volitions. In his reading of Balzac, Hawthorne did not augment his repertory of symbols and motivational ideas, but he did find confirmation of the opinion that "in this world we are the things of a moment, and are made to pursue momentary things, with here and there a thought that stretches mistily towards eternity, and perhaps may endure as long."[18]

In *Melmoth Converted* (1825), which is superficially dedicated to the purpose of refuting Maturin's thesis that no one will deliberately sell his soul to the devil, Balzac examines the issue of re-

nounced salvation on practically every level of society. One single
truth emerges from his investigations: man lacks both the intellectual and the emotional equipment to cope with the problem of
unrestricted desire. Whether it is John Melmoth or one of the persons who buy his privileges at their terrifying price, he can find no
peace of mind because he has no faith to bolster his belief in the
intrinsic value of ideals: "[Melmoth] seemed to have within him
a devouring principle which it was impossible for him to satisfy.
. . . his piercing glance, which read men's minds, would not waver
for an instant, nor his pitiless logic, which always seemed to go to
the very root of things. There was in him . . . the fierce and tran-
quil majesty of the tiger."[19] The powers of a Faust change the relations that formerly existed between the world and himself. He has
a vision of the infinite which makes it impossible for him to regard
human affairs as other men do. He has lost touch with the reassur-
ing foibles of humanity. Though his mind encompasses the mysteries of the macrocosm, his heart longs for the commonplaces of
the little world. He has inadvertently and unknowingly isolated
himself from mankind:

His lips glowed with desire . . . and he panted for the UN-
KNOWN, for he knew everything. Being permitted to see the
active principle and mechanism of the world, he ceased to admire
their results, and soon manifested that contempt which makes the
man of superior mold like a sphinx who knows everything, sees
everything, and remains silent and unmoved. . . . Rich in the possession of the whole earth . . . wealth and power no longer had
any meaning for him. He experienced that ghastly depression at-
taching to supreme power which only God and Satan overcome by
an activity of which they alone possess the secret.[20]

Upon consideration he realizes that mediocrity or dismal failure is
preferable to the self-sufficient mind. He longs for the humble faith
that once he had in the religion of his ancestors, and for the prayer
that seems to satisfy some deep and hidden need of his soul. In this
way Balzac exposes the fallacy of the superman; he proposes the
"unknown" as the necessary condition of human existence — the

source, as it were, of the dreams which later merge into man's ideals of perfection.

In *The Quest for the Absolute* (1834) Balzac portrays a bourgeois Faust. A nobleman, Baron Clues, is obsessed with the notion that he can extract from nature the secret of alchemy. Balzac develops this idea into a middle-class tragedy: the dire consequences of an overmastering delusion that destroys the peace and security of a conventional but highly esteemed family. As his wife perceives that their fortune is fast dissipating in costly experiments, she indignantly warns her husband that he is being faithless to his religion: "You are committing the sin of pride, of which Satan was guilty. You encroach upon God's prerogatives."[21] Her reaction typifies the reaction common to her class, and determines the tone of the story. The members of her circle, who collectively echo her opinion, are completely materialistic, incapable of the imaginative sympathies that might tolerate the ambitions of Baron Clues. Thus, Baron Clues, like all his Faustian counterparts, is alienated from the world in which his family and friends live; his limited Faustian ambition clashes with the conventions of society. On the other hand, as Balzac implies, the persistent quest for the secrets of nature hints at the danger which attends the repudiation of accepted moral standards. Contact with magic, to the degree that it obscures social responsibility, symbolizes moral deterioration, the sacrifice of spiritual to intellectual values.

The bizarre symbol of a piece of magic parchment measures the duration of a compact with the devil in Balzac's *The Magic Skin* (1831). At the moment the parchment shrinks into nothingness, the demon may claim the soul of the hero of the story. The fantastic device allows Balzac to dramatize the anxiety and suffering which overwhelm Raphael, a young writer, who enters into the bargain. Gifted with a powerful intellect and a sensitive imagination, Raphael at first takes his strange position for granted, being capable of assimilating his new experiences. Finally the truth dawns that he is living in a fool's paradise, and he cannot reconcile himself to the damnation which he conjectures: "Recoiling in horror from the fate of Faust,

he suddenly invoked Heaven."[22] Contemplating the newly awakened faculties of his mind, he finds them "eaten by gangrene, putre-
fied; the Devil had stamped . . . [his] brow with the print of his
cloven hoof." Surveying the complacency of scientific thought —
modern magic — Raphael, in the light of his own experience, begins
to realize that many mysteries of life defy the investigations of the
microscope and the telescope. Certain invisible realities lie beyond
the grasp of curious minds; totality of physical or moral truth is
pure vanity: "At the bottom of medical science — and the same is
true of all sciences — lies negation."[23] The overbalance of the rational faculties, the intoxicating joy of being able to visualize the
destiny of phenomena through an equation or a formula, generates
an indifference to human fate. In this state, a dispassionate force
tyrannizes the soul; Raphael suddenly concludes that "possession of
power, however great it may be, does not carry with it the knowledge of how to use it."[24] Again Balzac trenchantly criticizes the
Faustian will to acquire intellectual supremacy. The privileges that
knowledge bestows are not exempt from the censorship of a higher
authority: the divinity of the human race allocates to no single individual the omnipotence of God.

Similar speculations inform Hawthorne's tales. In the peculiar
nature of the Faustian mind there is an emotional inertia that fosters
isolation. In "Rappaccini's Daughter" he puts his finger on the inherent menace of the modern magic of science. In "The Procession
of Life" and "The Intelligence Office" he belabors the solipsistic
negations of abstract thought that lose their relations with the concrete realities of the earth. Yet Hawthorne could not and did not
accept Balzac's thesis that the ideals which motivate the conduct of
his Faustian heroes are always self-destructive. In "The Artist of the
Beautiful" the zealous pursuit of perfection and of higher truth,
though it does not bring any tangible reward to its protagonist, is
the path to spiritual emancipation. Hawthorne did not believe that
intellectual stagnation preserved a necessary human status quo, for
such would have been the corollary of a blanket condemnation of
Faustian desire. In the thought or the act, he searched for the truth

"beneath it, . . . [its] agency in life, and [its] influence upon mankind"; his was a mind "before which the forms and fantasies that conceal the inner idea from the multitude vanish[ed] at once and [left] the naked reality beneath."[25] As a consequence of this attitude, he could not delude himself that any human institution, however perfect its function, was an embodiment of all human truth.

In this analysis of novels colored by Gothic threads of the Faust myth, no claim of inclusiveness is advanced. A complete check list of the Faustian-motivated romance, considering the vast flood of narrative literature that issued from the late eighteenth and early nineteenth-century presses, would constitute a vast and ultimately unrewarding task. Yet by a curious coincidence, the most popular and in some cases the most original works fall into the category under discussion. Many of these Gothic romances or Gothic-influenced novels seem to have been known to Hawthorne. *Vathek,* for instance, was most probably in the circulating libraries which Hawthorne patronized in Salem. His sister Elizabeth relates that he was a critical reader who "made an artistic study" of all the popular novels of the time.[26] A letter to Louise, another sister, reveals that he had cultivated a taste for Gothic literature. He enthusiastically praises Godwin, Maturin, and Lewis, remarking that these authors absorb most of his leisure time.[27] Balzac, whom he read in the original French, fascinated him throughout his life; he procured copies of the French master's works as soon as they appeared in print.[28] Hoffmann's writings were frequently republished in American periodicals, and *The Devil's Elixir* was reprinted in *Blackwood's Edinburgh Magazine,* to which Hawthorne had access in the Salem Athenaeum.[29] There is also a good possibility that Reynolds' novels were familiar to him: the Englishman wrote voluminously, and fed his material into the popular literary magazines of England and America.[30]

Hawthorne's direct borrowings from the various forms of the Gothic tale were restricted, it appears, to symbols; however, he was not averse to adapting and modifying general plot themes or certain technical approaches. His predominant interest in the symbolic content of the Gothic genre was determined by a narrative method that explored the significance, in a spiritual sense, of traditional symbols. The deepest experiences of man avoid capture in literal speech; only figurative language can convey their meaning. A symbol is an eloquent metaphor that attempts to recreate the reality of these experiences. Just as a ritual act, or gesture, or song in primitive myth is capable of expressing a complex segment of obscure racial history, so the symbol in the rational context of literary myth is capable of reproducing a similar impression, of recovering some lost rhythm that completes the harmony of the soul's life. More perceptive than other Gothic practitioners, Hawthorne realized that the devices of Gothic machinery were nothing more than immemorial mythic images whose function had been obscured by rational thought. Because of their inevitable supernatural character, they aroused a positive response in the ordinary imagination. They gave concrete embodiment to the most mysterious adventures of the human spirit. This feature of the Gothic symbol appealed to Hawthorne. Hence, when he invented his own symbols, he imbued them with a preternatural quality. Whether they came out of early Puritan history, like "The Gray Champion," or out of contemporary phenomena, like mesmerism in *The Blithedale Romance,* they embraced the awesome wonders of life. This element, though other factors are involved, explains Hawthorne's predilection for the mythic devil-image and the diabolic pact. The image dealt with man's most precious and mysterious possession, the soul, whose eternity could be menaced only by evil. Having had a radical function in Puritan moral thought, it was the bridge to Hawthorne's nostalgic connections with the Puritan past; and having had a long existence in the Christian tradition as the ritual expression of evil, it partook of the universal significance which was Hawthorne's test of truth. But the symbol seemed to attract him most because, as the nucleating idea of the Faust myth, it had proliferated not only a basic set of minor symbols but also an equation that promised the resolution of the problem of good and evil.

CHAPTER V

EARLY SYMBOLIC MEANINGS
OF THE PACT WITH THE INFERNUS

HE CONTROLLING MOTIVATION of the Faust myth, the covenant by which man sells his soul to the devil, appears again and again in Hawthorne's fiction. Yet in no single instance does Hawthorne actually represent a human being literally signing the pact with the Infernus. It is not typical of his art to reproduce accurately the pattern of historical experience or the outline of a plot which is imitated. In transferring his materials into the "atmospherical medium" of romance, he sought "to bring out or mellow the lights and deepen and enrich the shadows of the picture." In altering his sources he felt that he did not "commit a literary crime."[1]

In formulating his Faust myth he follows this procedure of re-creation. Symbolically the ritual act of commitment is implemented whenever a character in his stories, either in thought or deed, endorses a mode of conduct that violates the conventional code or infringes upon natural human rights. To indicate that an illicit state of affairs prevails, Hawthorne ordinarily invokes the mythic image of the devil. However, on other occasions the devil is represented by proxy: the prevalence of witches or magicians, or the practice of witchcraft or of magic, establishes the condition of diabolic government. Whenever physical objects assume supernatural properties, whether they be magic portraits or enchanted mirrors, the devil may be said to reign. Whenever there is an interference with the laws of nature, as in the recourse to an elixir of life, the fallen angel asserts his authority. All these conventions are associated with the bastard genealogy of the Faust myth and with precedents found in the Faust chapbooks, in Faust drama, and in the Faustian-motivated Gothic romance. Yet since the myth is such a plastic conception, any author has access to the prerogative of improvisation.

A close scrutiny of *Fanshawe* (1828), Hawthorne's first novel and first published piece of fiction, discloses his early interest in the ideal of supreme knowledge, the prize for which the Faust of the chapbooks and of Marlowe willingly bartered his soul. One of the inspirations which tempered the handling of the Faustian material came from the Gothic tale. The young author takes no pains to conceal his borrowings from Maturin's *Melmoth the Wanderer,* and he expertly welds them into the structural design of his own story. The epigraph to chapter eight is culled from Maturin's poetry, and it is in this section of the narrative that Butler's catastrophic plunge to death occurs, an incident bearing comparison with Melmoth's fate. The president of Fanshawe's college is named Melmoth. And the "mysterious and unearthly power in Fanshawe's voice" and "his bright and steady eye,"[2] evinced when he addresses Butler, the villain of the piece, are reminiscent of Melmoth's bearing when he stands before the terrified wretches to whom he offers the devil's contract.

Hawthorne blended these Faustian variants into his story, so that instead of writing a typical sentimental romance he wrote something quite different: a serio-comic treatment of infantile emotionalism. Numerous details of the characterization reveal that Hawthorne's imagination was wandering in the fruitful realms of the Faust myth. But without a clearly articulated symbolism the fledgling novelist, instead of boldly charting the illicit course of Fanshawe's studies, hints that the books over which the scholar pored are "like those fabled volumes of Magic, from which the reader could not turn away his eye till death were the consequence of his studies."[3] Though not specifically the "damned" tomes that led Marlowe's Faustus to his doom,[4] they symbolically presage the cause of Fanshawe's death. Nor is the ambitious Fanshawe able to suppress signs of Faustian intellectual superiority; the pride in learning is reflected in his countenance: ". . . it was proud and high, perhaps triumphant, like one who was a ruler in a world of his own, and independent of the beings that surrounded him."[5] But even though he is disdainful of the aspirations of the petty world, his mind is intoxicated by a "dream of undying fame."[6] Thus all Fausts are corrupted by their earthly ties, susceptible to the selfish desires of other men.

Perhaps the most interesting facet of Fanshawe's personality is the one that stirs up associations with Goethe's Faust. At the time Hawthorne was writing the romance, there seems little reason to believe that he had come under the influence of the ideas of the drama.[7] Nevertheless, Fanshawe's spiritual dilemma is similar to Faust's. He is disillusioned with the inadequacies of pure knowledge: "He asked himself to what purpose was all this destructive labor, and where was the happiness of superior knowledge. He had climbed but a few steps of a ladder that reached to infinity: he had thrown away his life in discovering, that, after a thousand such lives, he should still know comparatively nothing."[8] The incident which reconciles the youthful Fanshawe to his lot parallels the Gretchen theme in *Faust*. Fanshawe falls in love with Ellen Langton. Subsequently, when the girl is kidnaped, he manages to subordinate his egoistical absorption with his scholarship long enough to accomplish her rescue, exposing himself at the same time to almost certain death. To reward his heroism, Ellen offers to marry him so as to lead him along the quiet paths of happiness "from which [his] proud and lonely thoughts have estranged [him]."[9] After pondering the advantages of this way of life, Fanshawe refuses to marry the girl; he deludes himself into thinking that he cannot sacrifice her happiness to his own, which is ostensibly a dedicated pursuit of the unattainable ideal of supreme knowledge. But in resisting the natural attractions of love and happiness, "he had exerted the whole might of his spirit over itself, and he was conqueror."[10] Here is the first suggestion that Hawthorne is mulling over the idea of spiritual rebirth in terms of the conquest of self, of the ego that will not recognize its predispositions toward evil or its inverted and frozen emotions. Thus, without the intense moral conflict with which Goethe endows Faust's relations with Gretchen, the Salemite presents a romantic solution to a problem similar to that

of the drama. Through Gretchen's love, Faust is brought into contact with the basic ethical values of society; she teaches him that he
has moral and social responsibilities in the world outside his own
thoughts. This was the lesson that Fanshawe failed to learn from
Ellen, who consciously assumed the role of his spiritual guide.

That Hawthorne had long been aware of this issue is verified by a
piece of juvenilia that he printed in "The Spectator," a weekly news-
paper which he wrote for the family at the age of sixteen. "On Solitude" is a precocious judgment on man's natural destiny:

> Man is naturally a social being; not formed for himself alone, but
> destined to bear a part in the great scheme of nature. All his pleas-
> ures are heightened, and all his griefs are lessened, by participation.
> It is only in Society that the full energy of his mind is aroused, and
> all its powers drawn forth.
>
> Apart from the world there are no incitements to the pursuit of
> excellence; there are no rivals to contend with; and therefore there
> is no improvement. Perhaps life may pass more tranquilly, estranged
> from the vexations of the multitude, but all the hurry and whirl of
> passion is preferable to the cold calmness of indifference.[11]

Again, even at this early date, Hawthorne looks at life and intuitively decides that the fire of experience must condition the quality of
spiritual ideals. Indications are that in the seven or eight years elaps-
ing between "The Spectator" and *Fanshawe* he mused further on the
incongruities of human existence. As he formulated these ideas in
the plot of his romance, he identified the most complete state of emotional isolation with the quest for unlimited knowledge. In Maturin's *Melmoth* he found justification for this conclusion. But, unwilling to adopt an unequivocal Faustian thesis, he, without alluding
directly to the pact with the devil, equated superhuman intellectual
desires with evil; and by an oblique reference to the black books of
magic he attempted to impart a supernatural quality to Fanshawe's
studies. Only after the novel was published did he recognize that his
color symbolism of black and white was not a convincing medium of
Faustian definition. Thus this tentative sketch of a Faust myth,
adapted primarily from Maturin's masterpiece, was a bitter failure,

for neither the critics nor the readers understood his narrative intention. Its redeeming feature was the skillful manner in which Fanshawe's ethical code was delineated, for at that juncture Hawthorne's
creative imagination manifested its kinship with Goethe's.

"Alice Doane's Appeal" and "The Hollow of the Three Hills," two
of the "Seven Tales of My Native Land," were probably composed
concurrently with *Fanshawe*,[12] and they exhibit Hawthorne moving
more confidently among Faustian materials. "Alice Doane's Appeal"
is merely a sketch for a story, and appears to be a variant of Lewis'
The Monk. The literal plot gains its impetus from the basic impulse
of the Faust myth: the ritual pact with the devil. Through the
machinations of a wizard, Walter Brome is prompted to tempt his
unknown sister, Alice Doane, into sexual lust, and then is slain in
revenge by his twin brother, Leonard Doane. The latter, tormented
by the belief in his sister's guilt and burdened by the sin of murder,
also feels inclined to punish Alice. To illustrate Leonard's degeneration Hawthorne invokes the controlling mythic image. Leonard's
mind, torn by agonizing conflict, is dramatically envisaged as the
theatre of temptation; it is shaken "by dark impulses, as if a fiend
were whispering him to meditate violence against the life of Alice."
Stung by remorse, Leonard determines to learn the truth of Alice's
guilt from the lips of his brother, and visits the magician who originally sowed the seeds of evil. The murderer is granted his request,
since "the wizard . . . on certain conditions, had no power to
withhold his aid in unravelling the mystery."[13] At the price of his
soul Leonard learns the truth, for, symbolically, the Walter Brome
whom he murdered is the demonic secret self which yearns to commit incest with Alice. But even though his conscience figuratively
immolates a proxy villain, the primitive sexual desire still persists,
gradually poisoning his mind in regard to his sister. The final meeting with the magician imperfectly recaptures Leonard's unwilling
acknowledgment to his conscience that the devil to whom he has
sold his soul is his own bestial passion.

In this early tale Hawthorne advances from the generalized treatment of a facet of the Faust myth in *Fanshawe* to a positive experi-

ment with its central motivation. Under the influence of the Gothic romance, he invokes the ritual pact to reveal the satanic nature of evil thoughts that threaten to compromise moral integrity. From the haphazard probings into Leonard Doane's conscience-stricken mind the youthful author learns the value of the mythic image of the devil as a psychological symbol. This perception into the fluid nature of the image immediately enables him to divorce his imagination almost completely from the narrative methods of his predecessors. For in the composition of "The Hollow of the Three Hills" Hawthorne applies this knowledge, stamping originality upon the covenant with the evil spirits. And thenceforth the sources of his plots lose their identity in the blinding light of his own inspiration. Even though this particular tale contains the ritual invocation of evil demons for the purpose of obtaining otherwise unattainable information, the details of the fatal compact, which make this feat possible, are beautifully camouflaged. In desperation a young woman resorts to demonic intercession to learn the effects of her dishonorable conduct. The witch whom she interrogates grimly comments: ". . . be thou bold, and the daylight shall not pass away from yonder hill-top before thy wish be granted."[14] Thereupon the sinful woman, at the bidding of the witch, kneels, placing her head on the old crone's lap, and a prayer is addressed to the infernal lord. In a short time the suppliant receives all the news for which she bargained.

A symbolic interpretation of this ritual act is necessary for a logical analysis of "The Hollow of the Three Hills." Hawthorne is not rendering an impressionistic description of a witchcraft ceremony. He is exploring the symbolic significations of the Faustian covenant. He rejects a literal portrayal of the formal service, and substitutes its equivalent — satanic worship. In her kneeling posture the woman expresses her adoration of the devil, the devil in her own soul; and her consecration to the enemy of God is signified by the loose garment which dips into a sluggish green pool, an ancient baptismal fountain of the devil's host.[15] But the supernatural symbolism has still another function. It serves Hawthorne as a dramatic device.

Instead of examining her spiritual degeneration on a normal psychological level of existence, he projects her hallucinatory remorse on
the plane of the supernatural. Here the idea of the binding compact
with the devil merges with the woman's morbid preoccupation with
the effects of her sin to offer a symbolic interpretation of the nature
and operation of evil in the human mind.

This early phase of Hawthorne's literary career may be seen in its
proper perspective if the semi-autobiographical tale "The Devil in
Manuscript" is examined. Just as the story illuminates Hawthorne's
anger with unsympathetic publishers, it also reveals his topical narrative interests. Oberon, the hero of the story, observes that the
manuscripts which he is about to destroy are penetrated with the
dynamics of a single nucleating idea: ". . . how the hellish thing
[the devil] used to suck away the happiness of those who, by a simple concession that seemed almost innocent, subjected themselves to
his power. Just so my peace is gone, and all by these accursed manuscripts." Oberon further notes that his obsession with the theme is
governed by its pervasiveness in the literature of the civilized world:
"You have read them, and know what I mean, — that conception in
which I endeavored to embody the character of a fiend, as represented in our traditions and the written records of witchcraft."[16]
This remark is nothing less than a definition of a primordial image,
of an archetype, of an imaginative idea of evil that has in many
different shapes infiltrated the myths of Christianity to work as an
educative principle. It is one of the memory-images

which from earliest times enticed man forward out of his brutishness,
breaking down to a useful current the terrible high tension he feared
in all the life around him, making amenable the recalcitrant earth
and the dangerous spirits by mastering them in the imagination, promoting religion to control superstition; then speaking persuasively
to man of good and evil, personifying the warfare of his own divided
heart, foot by foot, cultivating its wilderness, again and again re-
claiming the ground that had been lost. . . . Emerging from the
collective mind and illuminating it during the centuries when there
was no other light, [its] task nevertheless was to set man on his feet,

teach him to walk by himself, no longer one unit in a living aggregate, but an individual human being. . . .[17]

In so far as Oberon's thoughts bear upon Hawthorne's writings, this same mythic image, in its chameleon disguises, animates the pages of "Alice Doane's Appeal" and "The Hollow of the Three Hills." And later this symbol that was created by the collective consciousness governs the intrigues of evil that consistently flow from Hawthorne's pen. Thus the singular and inestimable value of "The Devil in Manuscript" rests in the information that is presented regarding Hawthorne's virtual slavery to the satanic image and in the continuity of thematic development which it foreshadows.

In "Fragments from the Journal of a Solitary Man," which contains still other observations by Oberon on life and letters, Hawthorne speculates on the nature of human destiny, radically deviating from conventional religious opinions of immortality. The views expressed, to a considerable degree, clarify his preoccupation with the operation of evil in this existence: "I clung to earth . . . unable to imagine any but an earthly happiness, and choosing such, with all its imperfections, rather than perfect bliss, which might be alien from it. Alas! I had not yet known that weariness by which the soul proves itself ethereal."[18] And in so far as life has taught him, he continues further on, man, even at his most individual, must seek emotional reassurance from the sense of community, not community with his fellow-beings alone, but with whatever is living in the universe. As from those long dead, so from his living and dying man may learn "that the world is a sad one for him who shrinks from its sober duties. My experience shall warn him to adopt some great and serious aim, such as manhood will cling to, that he may not feel himself, too late, a cumberer of this overladen earth, but a man among men. I will beseech him not to follow an eccentric path, nor, by stepping aside from the highway of human affairs, to relinquish his claim upon human sympathy."[19] And in the spirit of his mythic image, which teaches that an understanding of evil is the pathway to good, he concludes that "nothing selfish can interfere with the

sense of brotherhood," for, having "a spiritual sense of human nature," he can "see deeply into the hearts of mankind, discovering
what is hidden from the wisest."[20]

Taken together, the pronouncements of "The Devil in Manuscript" and "The Fragments from the Journal of a Solitary Man"
encompass Hawthorne's general viewpoint, literary and philosophical. His working conception of the devil-image is based upon the
knowledge that wizard-lore has its roots in the cultural traditions of
European Protestantism, which in its exaggerated fear of evil perverted the original pedagogic character of the Luciferian metaphor.
In a review of Whittier's *The Supernaturalism of New England* he
displays his familiarity with the sources of his mythic imagery: ". . .
the forest-life of the first settlers, and their intercourse with the Indians, have really ingrafted nothing upon the mythology which they
brought with them from England. . . ."[21] Significantly it was upon
the dogmatic bosom of the reforming church that the Faust myth
was nursed into vigorous life; and with the most infamous representative of the devil-legend, the compact with the devil assumed its unalterable direction, establishing the indispensable *Urpolariat* of good
and evil that became a common motif in tragic literature and a no
less common Protestant sermonic text. In Goethe's *Faust,* as well
as in Hawthorne's Faustian formulations, this inflexible antithesis
finally breaks down. Thus the pattern of Hawthorne's philosophy
embraced in Oberon's journal composes the general outline of the
problems of human behavior and human destiny that he will dramatically analyze in the plastic shape of the Faust myth expounded
in "The Devil in Manuscript."

"The Maypole of Merry Mount," "Young Goodman Brown,"
and "The Gentle Boy" were written about the same time that Hawthorne was putting the finishing touches to *Fanshawe.*[22] Each of
the tales reveals Hawthorne extending the circumference of his
myth, intent upon reporting the degradation of his mythic image in
early Puritan times. Hence he invokes it in these stories to dramatize
the misapprehensions of evil which prevail. As he points out in the
headnote to the Merry Mount piece, the recorded facts of the New

England annalists on this settlement, form "an admirable foundation for a philosophic romance."[23]

Therefore he sets out to investigate the moral poles of two oppos-
ing attitudes toward life. His purpose is to isolate the inherent evil
in the dogmatic positions of the two ideologies in terms of response
to an awareness of personal evil. The hedonism of the votaries of the
Maypole is contrasted with the gloomy acceptance of existence as
an ordeal of temptation. The mirthful revivals of pagan ritual which
mark the festivities of the communicants of Merry Mount are deemed
by the Puritans to be fomented by the devil: ". . . the Puritans
affirmed that, when a psalm was pealing from their place of worship,
the echo which the forest sent them back seemed often like the
chorus of a jolly catch, closing with a roar of laughter. Who but the
fiend, and his bond slaves, the crew of Merry Mount, had thus disturbed them?"[24] Only the maliciously curious imp who haunts
Hawthorne's imagination discerns the devil simultaneously tempting
the two hostile groups. On the one hand, the conniving demon leads
the celebrants astray by beguiling them with the vanities of life,
perverting their reason and encouraging their irresponsibility. They
resemble Marlowe's Faustus in their desire to taste every tidbit of
sensual joy that comes their way. On the other hand, the fiend goads
the Puritan fathers into tyranny, giving them spurious interpretations
of the good their Bible teaches. The Puritan patriarch Endicott and
his followers on one occasion attack and capture a number of hapless masquers, and in tones of arrogant spiritual pride the hoary
leader denounces the sinners: "But now shall it be seen that the Lord
hath sanctified this wilderness for his peculiar people. Woe unto
them that would defile it!"[25] And as Endicott works himself up into
zealous anger, the sardonic demon urges him on to brutal extremes:
". . . bind the heathen crew, and bestow on them a small matter of
stripes apiece. . . . Set some of the rogues in the stocks to rest
themselves. . . . Further penalties, such as branding and cropping
of ears, shall be thought of hereafter."[26] When he turns his attention to the bride of the May Lord, who has only a short time before
been joined in honorable wedlock, Endicott sees in the lovely young

girl the writhing serpent of sex; perforce he grimly comments: "We are not wont to show an idle courtesy to that sex, which requireth the stricter discipline."[27] Thus, in the conduct of Endicott, Hawthorne reflects the insidious evils, simulated as virtue, which dominated Puritan morality: spiritual intolerance and a fear of sex that amounted almost to perversion. Yet Hawthorne held no brief for the followers of the Maypole; their indifference to the tragic responsibilities of life was not to be condoned. So Hawthorne's historical tableau becomes the stage for a scathing stricture on spiritual lassitude and spiritual hypocrisy. As attitudes engendered by the mocking spirit of negation, they fall naturally into the confines of the mediating diabolic imagery. Where authority is abused in the name of dogma, where natural rights are suppressed, where religion itself is blasphemed by revelry, there is the domain where the devil collects a rich bounty of sinful souls.

The problem which Hawthorne examines in "Young Goodman Brown" is the tragedy of doubt, and he ingeniously resolves it on a mythic level of reality where fact and fancy interweave. Its chief actors are neither Young Goodman Brown nor his wife Faith; rather they are the symbolic creatures of Brown's distorted moral conscience. Suspicion and distrust are their unrevealed names, and their genealogical ancestor is evil. The ubiquitous demon that hovered over the scene at Merry Mount is again present to precipitate spiritual catastrophe. And in no other place in his writings does Hawthorne so clearly delineate the Mephistopheles who shared sovereignty with God in the Puritan religion. Even in using the title of respect, Goodman, Hawthorne betrays an ironic touch. The given name of Faith is chosen with similar aptness. The Puritans denied the existence of such a human being as the *good man,* and there was nothing in their dogma to sanction the *faith* that there was. The belief in natural depravity almost rendered these components of their vocabulary superfluous.

Lack of faith, suspicion, and distrust typify Brown's normal reactions to life. When he is about to depart on a secret journey — incidentally, the ritual ordeal of sin — his newly wedded wife urges him to stay at home, but Brown derides her lack of faith: "What, my sweet, pretty wife, dost thou doubt me already, and we but three months married?" Faith's answer to this well-meant mockery dramatically foreshadows the future: ". . . may you find all well when you come back."[28] As Hawthorne hints, the purpose of Brown's night-journey is to meet an evil stranger who has persuaded the young man to enter into some dark scheme. En route to his rendezvous, Brown resolves to sever his connections with his acquaintance, and remain faithful to the virtuous Faith. When finally Brown arrives at the meeting point, he is greeted by the devil, whose identity is established by the serpentine cane he carries.

From this moment on Hawthorne dramatizes the manner in which the spirit of denial, the accursed principle of the universe, exploits Brown's lack of faith in Faith to darken forever the Puritan's soul. The crucial question involved is whether Brown has a deeper faith in good or in evil. If the young man can maintain his fidelity to the ideal of his wife, of his religion, and of his own moral integrity, then he can elude the clutches of the devil, and withstand the latent inclination toward evil which resides in his heart. But Brown is no match for the master of sophistries and delusions. After the devil destroys Brown's belief in his wife, the symbol of faith, the evil powers claim another disciple. Brown cries out: "My Faith is gone! There is no good on earth; and sin is but a name. Come, devil; for to thee is this world given."[29]

Driven frantic by despair, Brown imagines that he is standing before the baptismal altar of Satan's followers. The speech Satan addresses to his host is extremely important, for he proclaims a doctrine which establishes Hawthorne's intention in the story. The demon's pronouncement that "evil is the nature of mankind"[30] is identical with the Puritan concept of natural depravity, the fundamental weakness of Calvinistic doctrine. And it is this specific doctrine which Hawthorne criticizes in "Young Goodman Brown." The Puritans were so preoccupied with man's capacity for evil that they overlooked his predispositions toward good. This illogical emphasis, though sincerely practiced, bred only negations. Goodman Brown exemplifies the process. His faith in evil was stronger than his faith in good. The convictions diseased his whole attitude toward life. He was unable to accept the existence of evil in the world; hence he was not equipped, morally, to come to grips with life. He was another pawn of the prepotent demon who was as dynamic a force in Puritan religion as God. That Hawthorne preferred to project this perverted religiosity on the imaginative screen of the conscience in the form of a ritual exposure to evil gives us a glimpse into the extremely subtle mechanics of his mythic formula. Had Brown been able to surmount his temptation, to read the riddle of evil objectified in his ordeal, he would have attained to a knowledge of the good. But such is heresy in the codices of sectarian religions: dogma must be respected. However, the issue of injudicious doctrinal stress is not restricted merely to Puritanism; it is the universal Achilles' heel of all institutional religions. Only by localizing this problem in the area of supernatural conflict, where the pact with the devil is symbolized in a nightmare of satanic baptism, could Hawthorne objectively appraise its universal implications.

In "The Gentle Boy" Hawthorne again probes into the rigidities of sectarian pride. In the clash of Puritan and Quaker beliefs, religious intolerance and persecution are allied to the operation of the principle of evil: the plots of the devil furtively increase the sensitivity of spiritual egos. Hawthorne's appraisal of fanaticism, which takes into consideration its inevitable cruelties, also broaches a tangential question: the human isolation imposed by a new idea and the capacity of human love to bridge this isolation. In two speeches using the symbolic image of the devil, he stamps the curse of evil respectively upon Quaker and Puritan fanaticism. As the plot of the tale evolves, the curse takes material shape in the action. The "hellish" eloquence of a Quakeress, who sacrilegiously mounts to a Puritan pulpit to denounce her enemies, is aimed at the devil of persecution which incites the Puritans to inhuman cruelties: "And lo! the devil entereth into the council chamber, like a lame man[31] of low stature and gravely apparelled, with a dark and twisted countenance, and a bright, downcast eye. And he standeth up among the rulers; yea, he goeth to and fro, whispering to each; and every man lends his ear, for his word is 'Slay, slay!'"[32] When the Quaker fanatic silences her harsh flow of invective, the officiating Puritan minister declares his position in the matter. He denotes her impious usurpation of his pulpit an act motivated by the demon: "Get you down, woman, from the holy place which you profane. . . . Is it to the Lord's house that you come to pour forth the foulness of your heart and the inspiration of the devil?"[33] These recriminations, in each instance conceived in the spirit of intolerance and of diabolic incitement, confirm the pharisaical foundation of sectarian pride.

On the part of the Puritans, their aggressive piety develops into violent persecution. To show its malignant influence, Hawthorne, using the familiar symbolism of myth, reports its effects upon Puritan children. Spurred on by "the devil of their fathers," the "unbreeched fanatics" subject a helpless Quaker child to a severe pummeling.[34] Quaker reaction to physical tyranny assumes the character of passive resistance. The punishment visited upon the sect is rationalized to explain their exalted status in the eyes of God: "O Thou, to whom I have looked in my farthest wanderings . . . inflict not upon the bloodiest of our persecutors the unmitigated agony of my soul, when I believed that all I had done and suffered for Thee was at the instigation of a mocking fiend! But I yielded not; I knelt down and wrestled with the tempter, while the scourge bit more fiercely into the flesh."[35] The function of Hawthorne's devil-image now becomes clearer. He invokes it to dramatize spiritual pride among the Quakers and the Puritans, at which time it gives embodiment to the infernal forces of denial that guide the conduct of militant church groups. The image also serves to illustrate the form that negation takes. Though capable of humbling the arrogance of the spiritual ego, it instead works as an instrument of confusion which deprives the reason of its capacity to distinguish between good and evil.

Perhaps the most oracular enunciations that Hawthorne records in "The Gentle Boy" are incidental to the problem of religious persecution. By demonstrating the charity of spontaneous human emotions, as in the Pearsons' unselfish concern for a little boy, Hawthorne implicitly avers that only the simple love of mankind can break the isolation that new or strange ideas promote among men and nations. Bigotry and fanaticism are the roots of hypocrisy. So it is no wonder that in this tale the over-zealous defense of dissimilar ideas of the good is quietly transformed into the operation of a vicious principle of evil. By recourse to the mythic image Hawthorne conveys his belief that emotional inertia compromises the integrity of the soul, since it denies common human nature. The desertion of the good signifies that the powers of darkness have achieved a victory over eternal truth. Such has been the moral and historical lesson derived from religious persecutions down through the ages. Hawthorne restates this proposition in terms of American history.

In this earliest group of narratives, Hawthorne is tentatively exploring the moral values of the devil-image and the ritual bargain. Even in *Fanshawe,* where the mythic imagery is loosely defined, his inspiration is conditioned by the influence of the Gothic novel employing various Faustian motivations. In "Alice Doane's Appeal" he begins to improvise on the Faustian machinery of the Gothic tales in the tradition of *The Monk.* Beginning with "The Hollow of the Three Hills," Hawthorne proceeds to pioneer a new course for the Faust myth. He utilizes the ritual act of satanic worship to give a devil-possessed mind its own peculiar stamp of evil. In "The Maypole of Merry Mount," turning to New England history, he examines the ideologies of irresponsible optimism and harsh pessimism to prove that both are corrupted by the negativism of the infernal powers. Against an imaginary background of Puritan history in "Young Goodman Brown," Hawthorne employs the ceremony of satanic baptism as a ritual ordeal to investigate the destructive effects of a firm persuasion in the efficacy of evil, and at the same time offers a caustic criticism of the Puritan belief in natural depravity. Relying upon the multiple associations of devil-imagery, he illumines the denial of human love that characterizes religious persecution in "The Gentle Boy"; and he also exposes the spiritual hypocrisy implicit in self-righteous piety. Evidence that Hawthorne decided to formulate his own Faust myth is found in the semi-autobiographical composition "The Devil in Manuscript"; and in its companion-piece "Fragments from the Journal of a Solitary Man," he indicated that he was going to investigate those phases of human conduct that isolated the individual from society so as to determine their location in universal moral geography. At the outset of his writing career, this philosophical interest was focused on Puritan history, where sectarian pride was a virtual manifesto of severance from the aspirations of the rest of mankind. In the period of creative activity that followed, Hawthorne still cultivated the themes of New England in the framework of his Faust myth, but on occasions he ventured afield into the province of the comic myth and into peripheral zones of contemporary experience. However, in this stage of his artistic development he was not to concern himself seriously with the deepest problems of his own times. That was to come later.

CHAPTER VI

THE DEVILS OF HAWTHORNE'S FAUST MYTH

ITH RENEWED SINCERITY Hawthorne declares in *Twice-Told Tales* that the achetypal covenant with the devil most persuasively symbolizes the enigma of human destiny.[1] This statement occurs in "The Haunted Mind," a narrative that defines the creative patterns of Hawthorne's imagination. In a few words he unbosoms the secret inspiration to which he rarely alludes directly: "there is no name for him unless it be Fatality, an emblem of the evil influence that rules your fortunes; a demon to whom you subjected yourself by some error at the outset of life, and were bound his slave forever, by once obeying him. See! those fiendish lineaments graven on the darkness, the writhed lip of scorn, the mockery of the living eye, the pointed finger, touching the sore place in your heart!" As Hawthorne speculates on the different literary forms that the idea might wear, he stumbles upon an experiential equivalent in the spiritual state of the mind represented by remorse, where riotously cavort "the devils of a guilty heart, that holds its hell within itself."[2] And here presented clearly, for the first time, is the hypothesis of universal moral truth: ordeal by sin. This mythic conception, as he develops the ramifications of his Faust myth, will activate the plots of such tales as "John Inglefield's Thanksgiving" and "The Minister's Black Veil." When at times he feels that his preoccupation with diabolic symbolism reflects his own disturbed consciousness, he reassures himself by fixing his attention upon the realities of life to discover that "the fiends [are] anywhere but in [his] haunted mind."[3] In the parallel between human life and the inspiration

67

which he cultivates, he observes: "In both you emerge from mystery, pass through a vicissitude that you can but imperfectly control, and are borne on to another mystery." The point of view is singularly rewarding: the imagination "strays, like a free citizen, among the people of a shadowy world, beholding strange sights, yet without wonder or dismay."[4]

The prerequisite to a consuming interest in the lives of other individuals is a Faustian curiosity about oneself. Hawthorne discloses this attitude in "Monsieur du Miroir." His image in a mirror taunts him with the ontological mystery of existence. The confused inconsistencies of man's spiritual life, he confesses, must ever remain insoluble unless he can unravel the secret motivations of his own being: "I will be self-contemplative, as Nature bids me, and make him [the other self] the picture or visible type of what I muse upon, that my mind may not wander so vaguely as heretofore, chasing its own shadow through a chaos and catching only the monsters that abide there. Then will we turn our thoughts to the spiritual world. . . ."[5] If the sphinx in the mirror should deign to commit himself, then Hawthorne may legitimately probe into the multifarious expressions of human nature. He is not content to accept passively the limitations imposed upon his knowledge by God. Some uncontrollable impulse of his soul urges him to lift the veil that divine intelligence has dropped before his eyes: "A few words, perhaps, might satisfy the feverish yearning of my soul for some master thought that should guide me through this labyrinth of life, teaching wherefore I was born, and how to do my task on earth, and what is death."[6] Thus Hawthorne submits the thesis that man's spiritual unrest derives from his Faustian desire to apprehend the eternal truths of the universe. Though they forever elude the grasp of his intelligence, nevertheless they retain the ambiguous reality of the fleeting reflections that haunt the face of a mirror. But the Faustian soul will have no peace until it has realized its destiny, however vague its promptings, however illicit its quest. In "The Ambitious Guest" and "The Threefold Destiny," Hawthorne deals with the ironic configurations of this compulsive yearning; in "The

Great Carbuncle" and "The Prophetic Pictures," he warns of the moral perversions that attend desperate Faustian enterprises.

It is necessary to remember that Hawthorne was not morbidly serious, for in evolving his Faust myth he also investigated its potential of humor. He recognized that not all the foibles of mankind were worthy of moral consideration; yet, as he pondered them, he could not resist attempting their solution with the Faustian equation. In the lighter variations of diabolic myth, as represented in the didactic folk tale, he found his prototype of the puckish demon. This incomparable artificer, who was not at all interested in immortal souls, tempted his victims into laughably gigantic follies. Hawthorne first mentions the comic devil in "The Seven Vagabonds." The association is aroused by his meeting with a wandering fortune-teller and conjurer who "pretended to familiarity with the Devil. . . ." But so far as Hawthorne is able to judge, the scheming old man is only a shallow counterpart of the evil spirit with whom he professes intimacy. His mental and moral traits resemble those of a down-at-the-heel Mephistopheles: "Among them might be reckoned a love of deception for its own sake, a shrewd eye and keen relish for human weakness and ridiculous infirmity, and the talent of petty fraud. Thus to this old man there would be pleasure even in the consciousness so insupportable to some minds, that his whole life was a cheat upon the world. . . ."[7] This undignified disciple of the mighty Lucifer appears in "Peter Goldthwaite's Treasure" and "Mrs. Bullfrog."

Though Washington Irving's "The Devil and Tom Walker" is usually called the "comic New England *Faust*," on the basis of sheer humor Hawthorne's "Peter Goldthwaite's Treasure" perhaps has a more legitimate claim to the title. Peter is a crackbrained schemer, impatient of ordinary business methods. He trades only in bubbles and wishful dreams, the vast fortunes of legendary El Doradoes. He is at last compelled to pin his hope for riches on the tradition that his great grand-uncle once hid a fabulous treasure in the ancestral mansion, the last of Peter's possessions. Rumor had it that the uncle had acquired this vast wealth through a deal with "Old Scratch," but ultimately the devil had tricked the elder Peter by "some secret impediment . . . [which] debarred him from the enjoyment of his riches."[8] The heir chooses to ignore this part of the old wives' tale, and begins to disembowel the house, confident of uncovering untold wealth; symbolically he is emptying himself of all desire to live within ordinary society.

Throughout the remainder of the story Hawthorne uses the symbol of the roguish devil of the popular Faustian folk tale to amplify Peter's stupendous folly. Tabitha, Peter's witch-like housekeeper, tells her master that he ought to take cognizance of his uncle's bad luck, for, as the latter "went to unlock the chest, the Old Scratch came behind and caught his arm. The money, they say, was paid Peter out of his purse; and he wanted Peter to give him a deed of this house and land, which Peter swore he would not do."[9] In the process of the wrecking operation, Peter finds a charcoal sketch on the wall of a room which momentarily disconcerts him, for it is a pictorial embodiment of Tabitha's yarn: "It represented a ragged man, partly supporting himself on a spade, and bending his lean body over a hole in the earth, with one hand extended to grasp something he had found. But close behind him, with a fiendish laugh on his features, appeared a figure with horns, a tufted tail, and a cloven hoof." With an "Avaunt Satan!"[10] Peter puts an axe to "Old Scratch," convinced that he has lifted the evil spell held by the demon over his uncle's treasure. Not until Peter has demolished everything in the house except the kitchen does he find a large chest which holds the reward of his labors. But as Tabitha hinted, the devil was not to be tricked. Peter finds a useless fortune in old provincial currency — the emblem of his status in the community.

Hawthorne once again uses the symbol of the jesting demon to give "Mrs. Bullfrog" the moral that fraud begets fraud. Mr. Bullfrog, a fastidious bachelor, marries a woman who epitomizes his quest for perfection. She possesses charm, good breeding, and virginal innocence, besides a considerable sum of money. The bride is intelligent enough to reason that her assets constitute about ninety-five per cent of her attraction for Mr. Bullfrog. Immediately after the ceremony the couple sets off in a stagecoach for a distant town. As they are riding along, the vehicle capsizes. Mr. Bullfrog, who is slightly stunned, rises from the side of the road to go to the assistance of his lovely wife. But the person in his wife's garb has metamorphosed into a monster. Gone are the glossy curls, the elegance, and the gentility. Blaming the driver for her ruin, this strange creature, bald, hollow-cheeked, and toothless, belabors the unfortunate man with an umbrella to the accompaniment of blistering imprecations. Mr. Bullfrog is terrified. He fears that the mocking fiend is at the bottom of the troubled situation: "In my terror and turmoil of mind I could imagine nothing less than that the Old Nick, at the moment of our overturn, had annihilated my wife and jumped into her petticoats. The idea seemed the more probable, since I could nowhere perceive Mrs. Bullfrog alive, nor, though I looked very sharply about the coach, could I detect any traces of the beloved woman's dead body."[11] Shortly thereafter, Mr. Bullfrog is confronted with the unhappy truth that he has married an impostor; instead of a treasure he has picked up a bundle of artificiality which, according to the standards of innocent beauty, is almost as worthless as Peter Goldthwaite's outmoded currency. Mr. Bullfrog's spontaneous conviction that "Old Nick" was the key to the duplicity is figuratively confirmed. His wife is indeed an old witch with as much guile as the folk-tale demon. When her husband indignantly protests the imposture, she merely remarks that she still has her fortune. Hearing this, Mr. Bullfrog, somewhat abashedly, recants the ideal of perfection, and the devil of greed wins again.

But as skillfully as Hawthorne managed the less meaningful symbol of the folk-tale Mephistopheles, it was no more than an experiment in technique. Perfect control over his mythic imagery presupposed a knowledge of the ideas that it could embrace on every level of human experience. The follies of a Peter Goldthwaite or the duplicities of a Mrs. Bullfrog illustrated only the proverbial truths of the practical world; they could not preoccupy Hawthorne long. In the melancholy expression of the young Faust of "The Ambitious Guest" there was more to learn of the tormented human soul than in a thousand recitals of the petty aspirations of an empty-headed speculator of Goldthwaite's stature. The ambitions of the youth who is a chance guest in the cottage situated in the notch of the sublimely beautiful White Mountains are for Hawthorne an exemplification of life's bitter irony. Rising above the shallow desires of the masses, the ambitious guest cries: "But I cannot die till I have achieved my destiny. Then, let Death come!"[12] Not achievement for achievement's sake is his ideal, but an abstract ambition to leave "a glorious memory in the universal heart of man."[13] For this reason "he had travelled far and alone; his whole life, indeed, had been a solitary path; for, with the lofty caution of his nature, he had kept himself apart from those who might otherwise have been his companions."[14] The death that overtakes this proud, reserved Faust is as anonymous as his vague, high-souled ambitions. A sudden landslide sweeps down from the heights to bury him with the humble family of the cottage. Only he among the group dies unnoticed: an unheralded stranger, an uninvited guest. So Hawthorne depicts the illicit character of an overruling desire for fame that left its aspirant stranded on an untraveled highway of life. Without depending upon the dynamic archetypal symbolism, he pronounces isolation from humanity the inevitable doom of the eccentric Faustian soul. The author does not condemn the actions of the ambitious guest; as in "Monsieur du Miroir," he views them as a quest for the "master-thought," human nature in rebellion against the limitations imposed upon it by unknown forces.

"The Threefold Destiny" serves as a companion piece to "The Ambitious Guest." But Hawthorne in this story allows his mythic symbolism to operate overtly. Ralph Cranfield, who believes "himself marked out for a high destiny," imbibes the idea through supernatural means: it is "revealed to him by witchcraft, or in a dream of prophecy. . . ."[15] Three signs are to confirm the approach of these marvelous attainments: a heart-shaped jewel on the bosom of a maiden is to proclaim the discovery of the only woman who can make him happy; a hand, visible only to him, is to point out a mighty treasure hidden in the ground; and an extensive influence

and sway over his fellow-creatures is to be a harbinger of great
leadership. Ralph becomes a world-wanderer, but nowhere does he
encounter the fateful signs. When he returns to his native village,
he finds the illusive tokens; but they augur more modest achievements than he had hoped. He accepts his prophetic destiny, adjust-
ing his wild Faustian dreams to the commonplace duties of those
precincts in which he had been born.

In neither of these tales of high-destined individuals does Hawthorne extend the outline of his myth. Though aware of the spiritual tensions generated by overweening ambition, he loses dramatic
impact by his failure to give them expression. The conflict with
conventional mores prevails only by implication, or is given a romantic solution, as in *Fanshawe.* The symbolic pursuits excite moral
platitudes, not philosophical truths. But as he writes in "The Threefold Destiny," he is still experimenting with "the spirit and mechanism" of legend or myth, searching for the incidents, "the characters
[and] manners of familiar life" to embody in the form.[16]

When symbol and idea perfectly balance, as in "The Prophetic
Pictures," Hawthorne assumes the role of a moral philosopher. The
mysterious painter of this tale is the counterpart of Leonardo da Vinci,
the Italian Faust, who "chose rather to know than to be, and that
curiosity led him within forbidden portals."[17] Not only does Hawthorne's painter excel in his peculiar art, but he "possesses vast ac-
quirements in all other learning and science."[18] His most astounding
gift, deriving from his prodigious knowledge, is the awful power to
delineate in a picture not merely his subject's features but his mind
and heart. Hawthorne, in this instance mentally attuned to the har-
monies of his Faustian imagery, ascribes this talent to intercourse
with the devil. Pious New Englanders inveigh against this rare pictorial skill: "Some deemed it an offense against the Mosaic law, and
even a presumptuous mockery of the Creator. . . . Others, fright-
ened at the art which could raise phantoms at will, and keep the
forms of the dead among the living, were inclined to consider the
painter as a magician, or perhaps the famous Black Man, of old
witch times, plotting mischief in a new guise."[19] Yet the painter is

indifferent to public opinion. What his art reveals he accepts dis-
passionately. He displays no more interest in a sitter than a scientist
does in a specimen to be dissected. Each flaw of character that he is
able to portray adds but another objective fact to his knowledge
of human nature. This intellectualization of emotion is severely
criticized by Hawthorne. Aloofness from the ordinary feelings of
mankind is a patent evil: "Like all other men around whom an
engrossing purpose wreathes itself, he was insulated from the mass
of human kind. He had no aim — no pleasure — no sympathies —
but what were ultimately connected with his art. . . . he did not
possess kindly feelings; his heart was cold; no living creature could
be brought near enough to keep him warm."[20] In this fatal inadequacy, Hawthorne discovers the fallacy of the Faustian superman.
Deliberate isolation from the common aspirations of the human
heart he considers a breach of universal morality. When knowledge
becomes an end in itself, divorced from the public good, it takes on
the function of evil. It ceases to seek a verification of its ethics in
the external world, being a law unto itself: "It is not good for man
to cherish a solitary ambition. Unless there be those around him by
whose example he may regulate himself, his thoughts, desires, and
hopes will become extravagant, and he the semblance, perhaps the
reality, of a madman. Reading other bosoms with an acuteness
almost preternatural, the painter failed to see the disorder of his
own."[21] Translated into the values of the devil-image, the diabolic
portraiture of the artist, in its failure to direct his spiritual government, merely corroborates the thesis that the evil of the ego-con-
sciousness is the inability of this presumptuous faculty to think itself
capable of wrong.

In "The Prophetic Pictures" Hawthorne realizes the full ethical
potential of Faustian mythmaking. The supernatural endowments
of the painter, attributed to intercourse with the devil, bring the
hero into contact with the inherent capacity for evil which every
individual possesses. In transmitting these secrets to the canvas, literally the lineaments of a devil–image, the painter himself fails to
heed the counsel with self which they urge. He is oblivious to his

own evil instincts because his ego overrules all responsibility to the community; for the image which he surveys is, after all, a communal symbol whose ethical purpose eludes him. He has divorced himself, emotionally, from his human heritage. On another level of the story, Hawthorne focuses on still another inadequacy of Puritan morality. He condemns his forefathers' intolerance of art, their fear that it encroached upon God's prerogatives; and indirectly he deplores their suspicion of the beautiful in painting, the only ideal that momentarily exalts man to the status of a god. And in equating the beautiful with infernal conjuration, they were exposing to public gaze the deserts of their souls over which the hot breath of the devil blew in fiendish glee. They, too, were blind to their devil-thoughts.

The fabulous jewel of "The Great Carbuncle" embraces the idea of a quest as infamous as the painter's pursuit of dispassionate knowledge. But the search for the carbuncle enables Hawthorne to broaden the canvas of his narrative picture. With the possible exception of the young couple, each individual participating in the adventure is motivated by a desire that reflects a specific phase of universal human conduct. Hawthorne is therefore allowed to pass moral judgment on their actions. Because "the quest for the Great Carbuncle is deemed little better than a traffic with the Evil One," doing "grievous wrong to [the] soul [and] body, . . ."[22] Hawthorne's symbol acquires its necessary mythic connotations.

The story, in relation to Hawthorne's development of his Faust myth, shows him widening the periphery of meaning of his conceptual pattern. The motives inciting the different adventurers gain his strong disapprobation. He censures mere romantic pursuit, vain and directionless ambition; the pride of the scientist who sees the carbuncle as a "prize . . . reserved to crown [his] scientific reputation; . . ." the selfishness of a merchant who thinks only of "the marketable value of the true gem"; the egotism of the poet who believes its radiance will be diffused through his works, establishing "the splendor" of his "intellectual powers"; the haughtiness of the nobleman who deems the carbuncle the only fitting "ornament for the great hall of [his] ancestral castle"; the cynicism of the dis-

believer who wishes to prove that the legend of the great carbuncle
"is all a humbug."[23] At the end only the couple prove themselves
"so simply wise as to reject [the] jewel" because it "would have
dimmed all earthly things" by its splendor.[24] Thus Hawthorne
contemptuously dismisses all forms of human activity actuated by
vanity, selfishness, or pride. In the process he casts the net of his
Faust myth into the deeper waters of mankind's experiences.

The two historical tales "Edward Randolph's Portrait" and "Lady
Eleanore's Mantle" present another variant of the Faust myth. Hawthorne this time utilizes the symbolic pact with the devil to magnify
political tyranny in the American colonies. In the first story the
portrait of Randolph, who obtained the repeal of the first provincial
charter, is the symbol of the people's curse on all irresponsible rulers.
The action begins with the provincial governor meditating an op-
pression against the inhabitants of old Boston. As he sits at his
desk, momentarily reluctant to add his signature to the document
that will implement the offense, his eyes scrutinize Randolph's portrait. A military aide, noticing the governor's curiosity, volunteers
to relate the history of the dark canvas. His recital introduces the
connection between the devil and political injustice: "One of the
wildest, and at the same time the best accredited, accounts, stated
it to be an original and authentic portrait of the Evil One, taken at
a witch meeting near Salem; and that its strong and terrible resemblance had been confirmed by several of the confessing wizards and
witches, at their trial, in open court. It was likewise affirmed that a
familiar spirit or demon abode behind the blackness of the picture,
and had shown himself, at seasons of public calamity, to more than
one of the royal governors."[25] The governor ridicules the story as a
fantasy. And when his niece chides his skepticism, he harshly announces his intention of putting the city under martial law. One
of the representatives of the people urges him to rescind the order,
warning, "If you meddle with the devil, take care of his claws!"[26]

Angered by these threats against royal authority, the governor
seizes the pen, resolved to sign his name to the paper that will put
his orders into execution. A provincial captain calls his attention

to Randolph's portrait, and he lifts his eyes to scan it. The governor
stares at it aghast. His aide's tale begins to materialize: "The expression of the face . . . was that of a wretch detected in some
hideous guilt, and exposed to the bitter hatred and laughter and
withering scorn of a vast surrounding multitude. There was the
struggle of defiance, beaten down and overwhelmed by the crush-
ing weight of ignominy. The torture of the soul had come forth
upon the countenance. It seemed as if the picture . . . threw its
evil omen over the present hour."[27] The governor, however, stub-
bornly persists in enforcing his will. Casting a second glance of
defiance at the picture, he affixes his signature. The rumors flowing
from this crucial meeting relate that his name was scrawled in
"characters that betokened it a deed of desperation. . . . Then, it
is said, he shuddered, as if that signature had granted away his salvation."[28] With ineffable ingenuity, Hawthorne deepens the significance of a historic moment in New England culture, giving it
an unforgettable emphasis by equating political dictatorship with
the loss of salvation: the signing away of one's soul to the devil.
And again the mythic image is evoked to direct and guide individual
human behavior, but aristocratic pride prohibits its lesson to prevail.
The governor refuses to take counsel with the evil that divides his
heart.

The pride of Lady Eleanore Rochcliffe in the second of the stories
symbolizes the hell-inspired harshness of the British agents ruling
the American colonies. By retelling history with this pardonable
democratic bias, Hawthorne succeeds in representing the courage
that went into the founding of the republic. Haughtily conscious of
her heredity and personal advantages as a relative of the royal governor of Massachusetts, Lady Eleanore places herself above the
sympathies of the common nature which binds together human
souls. This scornful attitude, coupled with an extraordinary loveliness, is ascribed to supernatural influences by the ladies of the province. The article that sets off her irresistible charms is an embroi-
dered mantle "which had been wrought by the most skillful artist
in London, and possessed even magical properties of adornment."[29]

To re-enforce the impression of Lady Eleanore's Luciferian pride, Hawthorne foreordains the dark fate that will smite her soul. One of her rejected lovers, a colonial youth of unimportant birth and no fortune, insanely importunes her to drink consecrated wine to prove her human ties: ". . . in requital of that harm, if such there be, and for your own earthly and heavenly welfare, I pray you to take one sip of this holy wine, and then to pass the goblet round among the guests. And this shall be a symbol that you have not sought to withdraw yourself from the chain of human sympathies — which whoso would shake off must keep company with fallen angels." When she refuses to do his bidding, the youth presents another strange petition to the arrogant woman: "It was no other than that she should throw off the mantle, which, while he pressed the silver cup of wine upon her, she had drawn more closely around her form, so as almost to shroud herself within it."[30] But still she will not relinquish this other talisman of her superiority.

When shortly thereafter a small-pox epidemic breaks out in the colony, the source of the dreadful plague is traced back to Lady Eleanore's mantle. Now the residents of the region find confirmation of their belief that the diseased mantle was the devil's banner: "The people raved against the Lady Eleanore, and cried out that her pride and scorn had evoked a fiend, and that, between them both, this monstrous evil had been born."[31] And soon the pride which brought the downfall of the mighty Lucifer and his most ardent disciple, Faust, also reduces Lady Eleanore to shame and to ruin. Her lovely face is blasted by the horrible scourge. Her lunatic suitor, whose very name Helwyse apparently provides a foreknowledge of her doom, insanely pronounces her elegy: "All have been her victims! Who so worthy to be the final victim as herself?"[32] And with this homonymic symbol Hawthorne concludes another historical tale whose macabre tension derives from the fire and brimstone of his devil-image. The poetic liberties that he takes with historical data are equally determined by art and by personal democratic conviction. The pride evinced by Lady Eleanore, with its immovable cruelty and heartless indifference, was for Hawthorne the emotional and intellectual index of British imperialism and, in historical perspective, of all conquering powers. In the light of his artistic method, nothing could project abuse of authority more clearly than the functional imagery of his plastic Faust myth. He had used it to ferret out the evils of Puritanism in "The Maypole of Merry Mount" and other tales, in one way; now, in another manner, he applied it to enhance the heroic courage of the founding fathers in their struggle with the evils of monarchical persecutions.

"The devils of the guilty heart," upon whom Hawthorne mused in "The Haunted Mind," are his subject in "John Inglefield's Thanksgiving." Here he studies the war between good and evil raging continually in the guilty conscience, and he focuses once more on the educative image of the devil, in this instance on a negative reaction. The dilemma in which Prudence Inglefield finds herself has its parallel in the Faust chapbook and in Marlowe's *Faustus*. The chapbook Faust, though he wants to repent, will not repent: "In this perplexity lay this miserable Doctor Faustus, having quite forgot his faith in Christ, never falling to repentance truly, thereby to attain the grace and holy spirit of God again, the which would have been able to have resisted the strong assaults of Satan; for although he had made him a promise, yet he might have remembered through true repentance sinners come again into the favour of God."[33] Hawthorne does not merely report Prudence's fleeting impulse toward repentance. He presents it as a concrete action, having reality in time and place. In the theatre of her conscience occurs her struggle with the devil, actually the attempt to school herself to a genuine understanding of the mythic image which her conscience invokes to warn her of evil. On the evening of Thanksgiving Day, in the midst of dissolute revelry, Prudence suddenly remembers the pious celebrations of her innocent youth. She re-creates in her imagination what would take place if she were now to visit the fireside circle. She envisions a cool welcome, with family affection growing in warmth the longer she stays. When her mind turns to the hour of domestic worship, her heart suddenly yearns for this solace. For a moment she is on the verge of repentance. But in this crisis she is intimidated by the demonic image of the devil which rises to her consciousness: "But her face was so changed that they hardly recognized it. Sin and evil passions glowed through its comeliness, and wrought a horrible deformity; a smile gleamed in her eyes, as of triumphant mockery, at their surprise and grief."[34] At the sight of their unhappiness, Prudence dares to challenge the negative power of the devil–image: ". . . her countenance wore almost the expression as if she were struggling with a fiend, who had power to seize his victim within the hallowed precincts of her father's hearth."[35] But, as with Faustus, she lacked the conviction of faith in God, and her volition was strangled by the overpowering challenge to her spirit. In this narrative Hawthorne, by recourse to the oneiric symbols of myth and by constructing an other-worldly domain of myth, succeeds in achieving the dramatic persuasion of similar scenes in Marlowe's *Faustus*. By conceding the reality of the invisible world of the conscience, he presents good and evil as the chief actors in the kaleidoscope of individual human experience.

The sharp-toothed devils of remorse that gnaw at Mr. Hooper's conscience in "The Minister's Black Veil" are symbolized in the black veil, which is the physical emblem of his secret sin. As Hawthorne develops the meaning of the veil, he denotes it the sign of the parson's bondage to the devil: ". . . catching a glimpse of his figure in the looking-glass, the black veil involved his own spirit in the horror with which it overwhelmed all others. His frame shuddered, his lips grew white, he spilt the untasted wine upon the carpet, and rushed forth into the darkness."[36] Here Hawthorne merely gives tangible embodiment to the general idea of the devils of the guilty conscience which he discussed in "The Haunted Mind," transforming the mythic devil-image into the shape the plot of his tale demands. On another occasion he confirms this transmutation, for he remarks that behind the crepe veil "ghost and fiend consorted" with Mr. Hooper. To enforce this impression further, he notes that "among all its bad influences" it had only one good result: "By the aid of his mysterious emblem . . . he became a man of awful power over souls that were in agony for sin."[37]

In this extremely subtle fashion Hawthorne repeats the moral import of "Young Goodman Brown." The over-emphasis on sin obscures the possibilities of good in the human soul. Mr. Hooper's
claim that every individual "loathsomely treasur[es] up the secret
of his sin . . ."[38] is an indictment of no one but himself. In effect,
Hawthorne states that a minister, as a human agent of God, is not
supposed to flaunt the power of Lucifer. His mission is to guide
both the pure and the sinful along the path to righteousness. He
must demonstrate the capacity of good which is inherent in any individual who dares confront evil, triumphing over its negations and
reading the sphinx-like mystery of the devil-symbol. The very veil
which ought to have guided Mr. Hooper to a new understanding of
spiritual truth distorts his mind, as a similar experience had affected
Goodman Brown.

That Hawthorne's attitude toward evil was going through a stage
of ethical refinement, consistent with the principle advanced in "The
Minister's Black Veil," is clearly indicated in "Fancy's Show-Box."
He grants that man is tempted into evil "by many devilish sophistries," since the fiend has "a wondrous power, and terrible acquaintance with the secret soul. . . ."[39] Nevertheless Hawthorne insists
that man's capacity for evil is overestimated: "In truth, there is no
such thing in man's nature as a settled and full resolve, either for
good or evil, except at the very moment of execution."[40] In other
words, neither human depravity nor original sin but rather the pres-
sure of circumstances and the confusion of purpose operate to promote the commission of sin. Such an outlook on evil is obviously in
direct opposition to the Calvinistic exposition of the idea. This stand
verifies the fact that Hawthorne approached the problem philosophi-
cally, not theologically. In terms of the Faust myth this philosophical curiosity is of even greater importance. It suggests that Hawthorne's ethical analyses are rapidly assuming the direction of those
in Goethe's *Faust*. Since both men were interested in evil only in
the narrow sense that experience with it awakened spiritual conflict,
they could determine the enduring validity of man's ethical ideals
by taking man's reaction to participation in sin as a positive test of

his moral integrity. If sin functions to distort completely man's prospects of the good, then he is indeed damned; if, however, he consciously admits his errors and thereby resolves to transcend them, he is admitting his responsibility to the unwritten laws of universal truth. In the specific sense of Hawthorne's art, the mythic image of the devil functions in exactly this way: it is the oneiric projection of the great racial memory that has endlessly mediated the problem of good and evil for man.

"Dr. Heidegger's Experiment" lays open to view another of Hawthorne's attempts to examine the individual's ability to profit morally as the result of a previous experience with evil. The elixir of life motif, as in Goethe's *Faust,* is the device Hawthorne employs to elucidate his problem. But unlike the playwright, he is compelled to resolve the consequences of temptation to further evil within the limits of a short narrative. All the magic paraphernalia of the play are reproduced in Hawthorne's setting. Faust's enchanted mirror is converted into a fitting ornament for Dr. Heidegger's study: "Between two of the bookcases hung a looking-glass, presenting its high and dusty plate within a tarnished gilt frame. Among many wonderful stories related of this mirror, it was fabled that the spirits of all the doctor's deceased patients dwelt within its verge, and would stare him in the face whenever he looked thitherward."[41] The witches' apes and the steaming cauldron that attend the preparation of the rejuvenating liquor are symbolically expressed by the doctor's black book: "The greatest curiosity of the study remains to be mentioned; it was a ponderous folio volume, bound in black leather, with massive silver clasps . . . and nobody could tell the title of the book. But it was well known to be a book of magic; and once, when a chambermaid had lifted it, merely to brush away the dust, the skeleton had rattled in its closet, the picture of the young lady had stepped one foot upon the floor, and several ghastly faces had peeped forth from the mirror. . . ."[42] Five venerable friends of Dr. Heidegger are invited to share in the experiment of rejuvenation. They, like Faust, have long since expended the vitality of youth. Before the scientist offers them the potion, he urges them to use their past experience in the event that the elixir produces the desired effects: ". . . it would be well that, with the experience of a lifetime to direct you, you should draw up a few general rules for your guidance, in passing a second time through the perils of youth. Think what a sin and shame it would be, if, with your peculiar advantages, you should not become patterns of virtue and wisdom to all the young people of the age!"[43] But once they have sipped the magical draught, they immediately revert to the conduct of youth. And in the exuberance of their revived energies, they topple over the container of precious fluid. The effects of the preliminary samplings wear off, and the five return to their dotage. In the spontaneous lapse of these aged people to the sinful behavior of the past, Hawthorne isolates the ethical problem broached in "Fancy's Show-Box." Even if the individual engages in evil once, he nevertheless can attain the good life. All he needs to do is to become conscious of his moral lapse. Dr. Heidegger's friends, instead of perceiving their errors, resolve to search for the fountain of youth. They fail to reap the truth that is implicit in evil. Only the old doctor, who does not bemoan the loss of the elixir, reads the lesson so vividly illustrated by their actions. In this way Hawthorne transforms the elixir of life motif of the Faust myth into an instrument of ethical clarification.

Hawthorne's two stories of the Shaker community in New Hampshire tentatively explore the fringes of contemporary life within the confines of his mythic imagery. This act betokens his confidence in his operative conception, and anticipates its later extension into the more critical problems of his times. The Shakers, whose religious principles forbade the practice of sexual intercourse, allow him to speculate on the type of moral rigorism that he associated with dogmatic Puritanism: in a word, with the spiritual pride which reflects the negative aspect of evil embodied in the devil-archetypes. In "The Canterbury Pilgrims" two lovers fleeing from the Shaker village are accosted by a group of pilgrims who, conversely, are seeking refuge with the sect. The pilgrims attempt to persuade the lovers to renounce their plan, pointing out that the outside world breeds only disillusionment. The young couple, however, are not to be shaken in their mutual faith. They are willing to accept "mortal hope and fear" as a substitute for a "cold and passionless security."[44] The truth that emerges from this story is simply explained: a religion intolerant of human nature is a worse evil than any its practices may seemingly thwart. In a Faustian context, the philosophy which subsumes this belief recognizes the sources of moral perversion in the denial of the natural man and in a complete surrender to evil. The inversion of emotions which Hawthorne condemns is what each individual's personal Mephistopheles fosters if there is no attempt made to circumvent his trickery.

The principle of moral cowardice is re-examined in "The Shaker Bridal." Hawthorne describes the evil wrought in family relations by an unthinking submission to abnormal dogmas: "One, when he joined the Society, had brought with him his wife and children, but never, from that hour, had spoken a fond word to the former, or taken his best-beloved child upon his knee. Another, whose family refused to follow him, had been enabled . . . to leave them to the mercy of the world."[45] But it is in the marriage of Martha and Adam that Hawthorne sees a travesty on natural morality. The couple, who are in the prime of life, are about to be ordained the temporal spiritual leaders of the movement. A mock marriage is to symbolize their consecration to the ascetic ideal. The despair which originally drove Adam to forsake normal existence has crystallized into a hard core of selfishness in the new environment. He has disciplined his emotions to the extent that they are now brutally impersonal. Martha, who joined the community upon the urging of Adam, has sustained herself on the hope that Adam, once rehabilitated, would return to the world of men and consummate their long-delayed marriage. But now that Adam has risen to leadership among the Shakers, his pride in the specious success has entirely divorced him from thoughts of Martha. As a consequence, when Adam signifies his intention to remain celibate, Martha dies, being unable to endure a desolate agony. Thus Hawthorne, in his first attempt to study contemporary life, castigates the diabolic negations of a current religious sect. In relation to his myth, he has progressively expanded its definition until now he is at a point in modern life identical with the one he had assumed in his examination of Puritan history. His moral objection to the negative aspects of Puritanism was the creative origin of his mythic conception; his first effort to adapt its motivations to the life that surrounded him is characterized by this coincidence of approach.

In summary it may be said that, with the statement in "The Haunted Mind" reaffirming his belief that all the evils of life could be balanced with the infernal pact of the Faustian equation, Hawthorne declared his intention to extend the outlines of his Faust myth. In "Monsieur du Miroir" he indicated that the peculiarity of individual destiny would engage his attention. And since human ambition is usually the most powerful influence in shaping destiny, Hawthorne, beginning with the rather vague and romantic motivations of "The Ambitious Guest" and "The Threefold Destiny," moved toward a moral clarification of the compulsive desires dominating man's nature in "The Prophetic Pictures" and "The Great Carbuncle." The humorous possibilities of the devil-inspired folk tale momentarily diverted him in "Peter Goldthwaite's Treasure" and "Mrs. Bullfrog." The dramatic value of the mythic imagery in enforcing the lessons of American history was skillfully realized in "Edward Randolph's Portrait" and "Lady Eleanore's Mantle." His concern with the insidious effects of evil upon moral volition in "John Inglefield's Thanksgiving" and "The Minister's Black Veil" reflected an attitude toward evil that was a necessary prelude to the dogmatic standpoint of "Fancy's Show-Box." No Faust myth, in the sense of the greatness of Marlowe's *Faustus* or Goethe's *Faust,* is possible unless the author holds to a definite opinion on the function of evil in the universe. In this latter sketch he adopted a Pelagian position: man, hampered by no deterministic principle of natural depravity, has the power within himself to overcome evil and attain moral truth. "Dr. Heidegger's Experiment" isolated the negative aspect of this issue, suggesting that the individual is prone to be overwhelmed by evil only when he refuses to profit by the counsel with self which it urges. The last stage of this particular development in Hawthorne's Faust myth found him tentatively exploring its practicability in appraising the moral values at stake in contemporary life. The Shaker stories, though they are tangential to the real problems of the age, anticipate the direction of his thinking in the next evolution of his myth.

CHAPTER VII

FIVE FAUSTS

AWTHORNE'S SHORT STORIES between 1842 and 1849, significantly coming after his intimacy with Longfellow, Hillard, and the Faust votaries of the Peabody circle, are notable for the creation of five different characterizations of a Faustian hero.[1] The distinct ideals pursued by these Fausts symbolize in one way or another the limitations of contemporary civilization. Hence these tales — "The Birthmark," "Rappaccini's Daughter," "The Artist of the Beautiful," "Drowne's Wooden Image," and "Ethan Brand"— become the medium of Hawthorne's philosophic criticism of life.

The presence of the five Fausts in this group of writings is no occasion for surprise. Many other tales and sketches of this period foreshadow the inevitable development of the Faustian heroes, at the same time illuminating the crystallization of basic ethical attitudes in the major works. In "P.'s Correspondence" Hawthorne observes that the thoughts excited by the ritual pact with the devil seem to transform reality into an "intolerably prominent illusion."[2] His subconscious mind is so sensitive to the devil-archetype that it automatically conjures a visible demon if he momentarily muses on other than concrete facts: "Death and fury! Ha, villain, how came you hither? Avaunt! or I fling my inkstand at your head. Tush, tush; it is all a mistake." But "odious wretch" though the ghost be, Hawthorne confesses that the simulacrum has long been "a kind of intrusive devil of a body servant" in his intellectual ivory tower.[3] Of the "uninvited multitude of shapes" tormenting the imagination of the "Man of Fancy" in "A Select Party," none is so

importunate as the tempting devil. This time he appears disguised
as an old witch, "a deformed old black woman": "This same black
shadow . . . now glided among the pillars of the magnificent sa-
loon, grinning recognition, until the man shuddered. . . ."[4]

Perhaps the clearest indication of the manner in which the mythic
bias of Hawthorne's mind tempers his writings occurs in "Main
Street." This imaginative recital of the important events in the history of his native Salem represents an attempt to interpret the hidden motives of human conduct. To explain the apostasy of the
confessing wizards and witches in the infamous Salem persecution,
Hawthorne constructs an ingenious "Faustiad." This device enables
him to give expression to the four great temptations which incite
Faustian desires: sexual conquest, illimitable wealth, boundless political power, and supreme knowledge. He attributes George Jacob's
intercourse with the devil to the promptings of sensual longing:
"[His] heart was empty, his hearth lonely . . . and Satan, in his
wanderings up and down, beheld this forlorn old man, to whom
life was a sameness and a weariness, and found the way to tempt
him";[5] he could not resist the attraction of satanic bacchanals with
their orgiastic lechery. Hawthorne ascribes the downfall of John
Willard, a struggling merchant, to a lust for vast mercantile power:
". . . the Black Man tempted him with great heaps of gold."[6] In
Martha Carrier's yearning to dominate the lives of other people, he
perceives the curse of her worship of the evil principle: ". . . the
Devil . . . looked into her discontented heart, and saw pride there,
and tempted her with his promise that she should be Queen of Hell."
He ascribes the unquenchable scholarly ambitions of the minister
George Burroughs to a flaw in his moral character: ". . . in the
very strength of his high and searching intellect . . . the Tempter
found the weakness which betrayed him. He yearned for knowledge; he went groping onward into a world of mystery; at first . . .
he summoned up the ghosts of his two dead wives, and . . . when
their responses failed to satisfy the intense and sinful craving of his
spirit, he called on Satan, and was heard."[7] Nothing recorded by
the annalists of Salem supports Hawthorne's reinterpretation of the

witch trials. In the peculiar Faustian direction of his creative mind is found the only logical explanation for this poetic extravagance.

When, in "The Hall of Fantasy," Hawthorne pays his profound respects to the "men in every age who . . . have been rulers and demigods in the realms of imagination and its kindred regions,"[8] his tribute to Goethe, the author of the immortal *Faust,* is more pointed than any he heaps upon Shakespeare, Spenser, Milton, or Bunyan. Standing before the bust of Goethe, he avers that the famous poet will survive forever. Others, the "crumbling relics" of ephemeral favorites, are in the hall; ". . . ever and anon . . . Oblivion comes with her huge broom and sweeps them all from the marble floor. But such will never be the fate of this fine statue of Goethe." His "transcendent imagination" will forever guarantee him his honorable position.[9] No perfunctory praise is this. Coming from a man who is usually reticent about his literary idols, these encomia establish more than a passing acquaintance with Goethe's *Faust.*

The clue to the nucleating idea that controls Hawthorne's characterizations of the five Fausts is contained in "The Intelligence Office." In this story, which offers an "epitome of worldly pursuits,"[10] he records those irrepressible desires arising "from the depths of [man's] nature."[11] Materializing in specific activities, they include all "the bustle of human business, the outcry of the jostling masses, [and] the rush and tumult of man's life in its noisy and brief career. . . ."[12] As listed in the intelligence officer's huge book of desires, these infinite yearnings are "enough . . . to make the good man shudder for his own wild and idle wishes. . . ."[13] In the petition of one of the visitors to the establishment, Hawthorne isolates what may be termed the germinal Faustian urge of every thinking individual: "I want . . . my true place in the world! my proper sphere! my thing to do, which nature intended me to perform when she fashioned me thus awry, and which I have vainly sought all my lifetime!"[14] But once the design of one's life is settled upon, then the danger begins. If one drives toward his goal with a relentless volition, his soul is inevitably doomed. Hawthorne illustrates this truth in the story of a poor, unfriended youth who resolved to become wealthy. Now an immensely rich man, he approaches the intelligence agent to dispose of his estate. He confesses that to acquire his utmost wish he sold his soul to the devil. Thus anyone who wishes to purchase his estate must assume this encumbrance. The Man of Intelligence assures him that such a transaction is out of the jurisdiction of his office: "I fear that no bargain can be negotiated on these conditions. Very probably the next possessor may acquire the estate with a similar incumbrance, but it will be of his own contracting, and will not lighten your burden in the least." Frustrated in his scheme, the financier, like Melmoth the Wanderer, must carry "the dirt of [his] accursed acres and the granite of [his] infernal mansion" as a weight on his soul.[15]

As Hawthorne astutely observes, the desire for gold is repeated with wearisome frequency, since "wealth is the golden essence of the outward world, embodying almost everything that exists beyond the limits of the soul; and therefore it is the natural yearning for the life in the midst of which we find ourselves, and of which gold is the condition of enjoyment. . . ."[16] The least prosaic of human longings are those incidental "to men who [have] gone deep into scientific pursuits, [or] attained a high intellectual stage. . . ." On this level of experience Hawthorne discerns both the tragedy and irony of human existence. Gifted minds enter into contention with nature, aspiring to "wrest from her some secret or some power which she [has] seen fit to withhold from mortal grasp." Yet there is no better way, Hawthorne concludes, to examine "human character in its individual developments" or "human nature in the mass" than "in its wishes."[17] In the struggle for their realization "more of good and more of evil . . . more redeeming points of the bad and more errors of the virtuous . . . higher upsoarings, and baser degradation of the soul" emerge than it is possible to witness in any other appraisal of human conduct.[18]

Hawthorne therefore proceeds to apply this yardstick of truth to the aspirations of his world. In terms of his myth the ideal pursued by his Faustian hero will symbolize a general phase of contemporary endeavor. In the success or failure of the quest, in the abuse or exaltation of the individual soul that results, in the implicit or explicit evil inherent in the chosen activity, and in the condemnation or the encouragement which the project arouses, Hawthorne's criticism of life will be evident. In a Faustian perspective he is on valid ground. Just as Calderón in *Il Mágico Prodigioso* expresses the yearnings of the Spanish Renaissance, or Marlowe in *Faustus* testifies to the *ethos* of the English Renaissance, or Goethe in *Faust* exposes the tortured aspirations of a century that has lost its faith in pure reason,[19] so Hawthorne in his five tales also unveils the powerful forces that were shaping the nineteenth-century American mind.

Exercising the conventional privilege of a mythmaker of being "allowed a license with regard to every-day possibility,"[20] Hawthorne, in "The Birthmark," presents a devastating indictment of modern science. In Aylmer's belief that it was possible to discover "the secret of creative force"[21] or perfection itself there is the equivalent presumption that marked scientific thought in Hawthorne's day. New developments in geology, as characterized in Charles Lyell's *Principles of Geology* (1830), and in chemistry, as evidenced by Benjamin Silliman's *Elements of Chemistry* (1830), held forth the same promise as Aylmer's natural philosophy. Man was at the threshold of a new era of thought that heralded infinite material progress. He was living in a world of almost supernatural achievements where ordinary human emotions and traditional morality no longer were meaningful.

Aylmer's obsessive desire to remove the flaw that blights his wife's beauty symbolizes the ruthless course of the nineteenth century. Though Aylmer struggles to recognize the authority of a law greater than his own talents, he does not succeed. Hawthorne visualizes his predicament as similar to that of Goethe's Faust: two souls are lodged in the young scientist's breast. One focuses its love on the wife, the other on scientific study. When finally the love of abstract learning conquers human love, Aylmer prepares to attempt a daring experiment to eradicate the birthmark on Georgiana's cheek. Though Aylmer rationalizes the defect in Georgiana's beauty as a symbol of

her liability to sin, sorrow, and decay, which, to glorify her perfection, has to be effaced, he in reality feels his scientific vanity threat-
ened: "[His] sombre imagination was not long in rendering the
birthmark a frightful object, causing him more trouble and horror
than ever Georgiana's beauty, whether of soul or sense, had given
him delight."[22] When she pleads with him to consider her emotions,
brought to the point of madness by his repugnance and disgust, he
ignores her complaints, enraptured with the dream of scientific attainment: "Georgiana, you have led me deeper than ever into the
heart of science. I feel myself fully competent to render this dear
cheek . . . faultless; . . . and then, most beloved, what will be
my triumph when I shall have corrected what Nature left imperfect
in her fairest work!"[23]

The girl's final statement to her husband signifies her willingness
to sacrifice herself to his science. Loving him with complete unself-
ishness, she, even though death is inevitable, chooses this way to
humble his ego. "Life is but a sad possession to those who have
attained precisely the degree of moral advancement at which I stand.
Were I weaker and blinder it might be happiness. Were I stronger,
it might be endured hopefully. But, being what I find myself, me-
thinks I am of all mortals the most fit to die."[24] The scientist fails
to heed her words. The experiment is rushed to its conclusion, but
just as it appears successful Georgiana dies. Thus the first of Hawthorne's Fausts, in a purely symbolic line of action sacrifices his soul
to conquer nature, the universal force of which man is but a tool.
As Goethe's Faust discovered that he was not the equal of the pervasive earth-spirit, so does Aylmer. In this fashion Hawthorne indicates that man's sphere of activity cannot extend beyond man; where
natural rights of the individual are abused, whatsoever the ideal
involved, the divine essence of humanity is profaned. Human emotions cannot be intellectualized with impunity, for they well from
the moral springs of the heart. This is the bitter truth, for better or
for worse, that every dedicated scientist must eventually learn.

In "Rappaccini's Daughter" Hawthorne denotes the deliberate
ethical indifference of modern science as the equivalent, symboli-

cally, of this Italian Faust's attempt to thwart human mortality with poison. Rappaccini, who "is as true a man of science as ever distilled his own heart in an alembic,"[25] is the epitome of moral insensibility. Typical of the scholar who pursues learning as an end in itself, "he cares infinitely more for science than for mankind. His patients are interesting to him only as subjects for some new experiment. He would sacrifice human life, his own among the rest, or whatever else was dearest to him, for the sake of adding so much as a grain of mustard seed to the great heap of his accumulated knowledge."[26] Possessing a theory "that all medicinal virtues are comprised within those substances which we term vegetable poisons,"[27] he cultivates a garden of poisonous plants, which are lethal to the very touch. In order to have some one to watch over them properly, he gradually inoculates his daughter with venoms which make her immune to the effects of the plants but at the same time as poisonous as they. When he realizes that he has unwittingly isolated her from normal human love, he insidiously subjects a young man to a treatment making the latter a fit bridegroom for his daughter.

Rappaccini's distorted belief that he has thereby rendered the two young persons insusceptible to all the diseases of mankind is the basis of his "pride and triumph."[28] In depriving them of common human intercourse and in making them a constant menace to all other living things, he shows himself incapable of apprehending the meaning of morality. For Hawthorne this intellectual perversion is what he fears and castigates. He perceives that a science which advances more rapidly than morals will create an ethical reality of its own. Once this condition prevails there will be no possibility of reconciling the values of science and those of Christianity. What he perceives is the controversy between science and religion that caused Emerson and others so much concern. The Italian Faust personifies the danger of dehumanization inherent in the egocentricity of scientific endeavor.

In thus condemning the quest for scientific perfection that blinds its aspirant to social and moral responsibilities, Hawthorne is not unaware that the materialistic aspects of his age are just as degrading to the spirit. In "The Artist of the Beautiful" Owen Warland's desire to create ideal beauty is symbolic of those eternal spiritual values, embodied in man's conception of the divinity, that the mercenary world is fast destroying. Therefore Hawthorne's portrait of Warland is an objectification of the Faustian aspiration of the artist: the desire to produce a beauty that "should attain to the ideal which Nature has proposed to herself in all her creatures, but has never taken pains to realize."[29] Yet the tragedy of the artistic life is not that man does not achieve his dream. The collapse of his dearest projects is the penalty of mortality. However, when society conspires against the achievement, then the human race has lost a precious legacy of dignity. The lack of imaginative sympathy is more discouraging than failure itself. Under such circumstances the lot of an artist attempting to give external reality to an idea is infinitely difficult: "he must keep his faith in himself while the incredulous world assails him with its utter disbelief; he must stand up against mankind and be his own sole disciple, both as respects his genius and the objects to which it is directed."[30]

In the characterization of Owen Warland, Hawthorne again adapts a Goethean conception of two souls residing in man's breast, the one clinging to the things of the earth, the other striving to attain its supersensual origins. Warland, who believes himself in love with Annie Hovendon, endeavors to enlist her support in his design of the beautiful. Annie, though outwardly beautiful, lacks the spiritual qualities which her physical being suggests. Instead of inspiring Warland, she retards his genius. She is a portion of the gross earth that curbs the flight of Warland's soul to its otherworldly ideal. But even more of a deterrent to his creative life is Annie's father, a jeweler for whom Warland works. Peter Hovendon's "cold unimaginative sagacity," the badge of the practical world, leaves Warland no peace of mind. The young artist believes his employer the devil who rules the destiny of the materialistic age: "You are my evil spirit . . . you and the hard, coarse world! The leaden thoughts and the despondency that you fling upon me are my clogs, else I should long ago have achieved the task that I was created for."[31] But the devil's gifts, which obscure the values of the spirit, are not easily rejected, for at last even the baffled youth surrenders his dreams to the mercenary god.

But once the artist senses that only faith in himself will enable him to prosecute his task to its end, he attains the purpose of his life. He conquers the sloth of inspiration induced by his ignominious capitulation to the world he loathes; out of the mire of indifference and of intellectual torment he climbs, spiritually reborn. He infuses a mechanical butterfly with the "harmony of motion [and the] mystery of beauty" which belong to the living species.[32] He offers this magnificent piece of art to Annie as a bridal gift. The girl who has married a man as earthy and practical as herself can hardly suppress her scorn of her former lover. But Warland is impervious to her reactions; he has reconciled himself to the inevitability of opinions like hers, which once would have endlessly tortured his soul. He knows that "the world, and Annie as the representative of the world, whatever praise might be bestowed, could never say the fitting word nor feel the fitting sentiment which should be the perfect recompense of an artist who, symbolizing a lofty moral by a material trifle, — converting what was earthly to spiritual gold, — had won the beautiful into his handicraft."[33] Subsequently, when Annie's infant son crushes the butterfly in his tiny fist, Warland is unperturbed. He has already gained his reward: ". . . the symbol by which he made it [the beautiful] perceptible to mortal senses became of little value in his eyes while his spirit possessed itself in the enjoyment of the reality."[34]

The implications of "The Artist of the Beautiful" transcend the simple theme of ideal beauty. To Hawthorne the idea of the beautiful is any inspiration exalted by the individual that will illuminate the life of mankind. It may be a philosophical system that has as its goal the reform of the world, or the message of a prophet, like Christ or Buddha, which will turn the thoughts of men inward toward an awareness of themselves in all their imperfections. But nothing, says Hawthorne in "Main Street," is less tolerable than a new idea of the good: "[It] has ever been most hateful to all other men, since its very existence seems to threaten the overthrow of whatever the toil-

some ages have built up. . . ."[35] Hawthorne considered the materialism of his times the enemy of fructifying ideas. Under the
impetus of the industrial revolution only practical ideas were held
tenable. In the symbolic overtones of this tale his criticism of ramp-
ant materialism and spiritual starvation rings out with unrelenting
harshness.[36]

The experience of the carver in "Drowne's Wooden Image,"
though similar to Owen Warland's, results in spiritual lethargy.
Drowne neglects to hold in mind the reality of the idea to which he
gave concrete form. Except in a brief interlude of inspired work-
manship, his sensibilities are as dull and impassive as his wooden
artistic medium. In him Hawthorne denounces the voluntary surrender to circumstance and standardization. And with marvelous
skill he symbolizes the carver's spiritual defeat in the devil of negation, an ancestral heritage. Given a commission to reproduce the
figure of a living woman, Drowne falls in love with his model, even
though he senses that she is unattainable. His imagination conceives
that her twin is imprisoned like a hamadryad in an oak, and he resolves to conjure her out of the secret dwelling place with the magic
of his cunning hands. As the statue begins to take shape, its beauty
is deemed sinful by the bigots of the village. They "hinted that it
would be no matter of surprise if an evil spirit were allowed to enter
this beautiful form, and seduce the carver to destruction."[37] At the
identical time that Drowne completes this wondrous figure, the living replica of it is seen to walk the streets. A Puritan of the old
stamp mutters his dark opinion on what has happened: "One thing
is certain, . . . Drowne has sold himself to the Devil." Other men
shake their heads and hint that their "forefathers would have thought
it a pious deed to burn the daughter of the oak with fire."[38] But as
mysteriously as the real woman appeared, she disappears. And simultaneously Drowne relapses into mediocrity. He becomes again a
creature of uninspired mechanical skill.

When Hawthorne invokes the image of the devil, his purpose is
to symbolize the disparaging demon of modern life that holds inspiration to be a thing of suspicion. The lifeless statues of Drowne's

mechanical deftness are the stereotyped emblems which excite perfunctory admiration and praise. They are signs of inflexible conven-
tionality, the hereditary quality of Puritan thought. During the
period when Drowne denies his slavery to the fiend of negation
lurking in the dark corner of his brain, his imagination leaps beyond
the narrowness of his environment. He attains to the lofty inspiration of his soul as love repels the influence of the spirit who denies.
But when he is unable to arouse a reciprocal passion in the figure he
has externally endowed with life and loveliness, he begins to doubt
his ability. The beckoning ideal of surpassing beauty passes out of
his vision, spelling the death of his genius. Great talent cannot content itself with the accepted standards of perfection. It must seek its
origins in the spiritual realms where values are eternal. Such is the
critical message of "Drowne's Wooden Image."

"Ethan Brand," a tale which Hawthorne describes in the subtitle
as a chapter from an abortive romance, offers the first definite evidence that he was contemplating the composition of a novel which
might have become the unchallenged New England *Faust*. Ethan
Brand is the great Faust of this period of Hawthorne's writing; even
though Brand's life spans only a short narrative, the implications
of his search for the unpardonable sin penetrate deeply into the social and philosophical foundations of nineteenth-century American
thought. The sin sought by Brand, a "mode of guilt which could
neither be atoned for nor forgiven,"[39] is a triadic symbol. As actual-
ized, the sin has no specific theological significance: it represents,
rather, the commission of the most abhorrent social evil, an affront
to the brotherhood of man, a denial "of the magnetic chain of humanity."[40] In its second aspect, the unpardonable sin denotes the
attainment of the one indispensable truth of human relations: Brand
learns that intercourse between man and man is impossible without
love, tenderness, and sympathy. These qualities are the chief ingredi-
ents of universal morality. As ethical principles, they are flexible
enough to cope with man's radical imperfections. In its last category
of meaning, "the one only crime for which Heaven could afford no
mercy"[41] is the philosophical equivalent of supreme knowledge.

The New England Faust discovers that evil is the natural outcome of man's tragic intellectual and emotional inadequacies. Thus, as an operative force in life, evil is not to be condoned nor is it to be condemned: it is to be understood as an unavoidable portion of human destiny.

In narrating the history of Ethan Brand's prodigious crime against mankind, Hawthorne reverts once again to the ritual archetype of the Faust story. To satisfy an inordinate curiosity about the nature of evil in the universe, Brand, whenever spared a moment from labor, invokes "a fiend from the hot furnace of [his] lime-kiln" in order to confer "with him about the Unpardonable Sin."[42] With typical indirection, Hawthorne mentions no compact between Brand and Satan, but later circumstances indicate that Brand sold his soul to the devil for the privilege of discovering the Master Sin. The demon, however, can acquire no legal mortgage on Brand's soul until he tempts him into sin. His diabolic purpose is to destroy this Faust's "pity for human guilt and woe."[43] This deed can be accomplished only by neutralizing the latter's capacity for sympathy: in short, by developing his intellectual pride. The vast knowledge which Brand subsequently accumulates places him irretrievably in the fiend's clutches. The sombre Faust loses interest in man's divinity: "He was no longer a brother-man, opening the chambers or the dungeons of our common nature by the key of holy sympathy, which gave him a right to share in all its secrets; he was now a cold observer, looking on mankind as the subject of his experiment, and, at length, converting man and woman to be his puppets, and pulling the wires that moved them to such degrees of crime as were demanded by his study."[44] And as the devil predetermines by expediting Brand's intellectual growth, it is only a matter of time before the unfortunate man is a victim of his own unremitting intelligence: he discovers the unpardonable sin in his own heart.

But what the devil did not foresee is Brand's reaction to this disillusioning truth. Though unconditionally doomed by his conduct, the former lime-worker does not bemoan his fate. The agonies of the present and the sufferings of the future are but a small fee to pay for the enlightening wisdom that has invaded his mind and soul: "Freely, were it to do again, would I incur the guilt."[45] As a consequence, when the devil, disguised as the Wandering Jew whose crime was also a denial of the magnetic chain of humanity, prematurely appears to collect his due, Ethan Brand sternly rebukes him: "Peace . . . or get thee into the furnace yonder!"[46] In the few hours of freedom that remain, Hawthorne's strong-willed Faust wishes to meditate on his sin, and to ponder his terrible isolation from mankind. His powerful valedictory to life, exalted by grief and remorse, expresses the deepest meaning of Aristotle's catharsis. With humility Ethan Brand confesses that his commission of the unpardonable sin broke the link connecting man with nature and with God. As a consequence, he is a homeless exile in the moral universe, having violated the immutable law of love: "O Mother Earth . . . who art no more my Mother, and into whose bosom this frame shall never be resolved! O mankind, whose brotherhood I have cast off, and trampled thy great heart beneath my feet! O stars of heaven, that shone on me of old, as if to light me onward and upward! — farewell all, and forever. Come, deadly element of Fire, — henceforth my familiar friend!"[47]

In Ethan Brand's reaffirmation of his belief in the magnetic chain of humanity, the noble creed which the devil sought to supplant with pride and selfishness, Hawthorne indirectly asserts his support of a philosophy that impinged upon the mid-nineteenth-century New England mind. Brand's conviction of "the sense of brotherhood with man and reverence for God"[48] is the message of Horace Bushnell and his followers. One of Bushnell's declarations is similar to the preceding statement by Hawthorne. Such perfection as man can attain will come with "the love of kindred souls thirsting after truth, and tracing back their way to that bright essence, whose image they dimly remember, and which, having cast its shadow on them . . . made them forever kindred to each other and to it."[49] And in the struggle toward this goal, man will go, Bushnell proclaims, through an ordeal similar to Ethan Brand's: "The perfectibility of man is forever excluded here, by the tenor of his evidence. He is here, in a flood of successive generations, to make experiment of evil, to learn the worth of virtue in the loss of it, and by such knowledge be at last confirmed in it. As long, therefore, as he is here, evil will be, and life will be a contest with it."[50] Whether or not Hawthorne was influenced by Bushnell is of little moment. However, Ethan Brand's life dramatically recapitulates the truth of the experience outlined by Bushnell: the ordeal of evil is the necessary condition of spiritual edification.

Just as assiduous as Ethan Brand's quest for the knowledge of evil was the Transcendentalists' search for the meaning of good. In this comparison the symbol of the unpardonable sin evolves into a subtle criticism of transcendental theory. Its exponents had seized the concept that the mind was capable of reducing the chaos of experience to a rational pattern of understanding. They had, in the process, discarded the category of the better and the worse in appraising human behavior. In reference to their ideal of a harmonious universe, evil was not a positive force in life. It was the negative expression of some great and eternal law emanating from the divine mind. This idealistic rationalization did little to explain or justify the tragic pageant of life. Hence Hawthorne held their speculative truths suspect. They had not established the supremacy of the intellect over truth. Disdaining this metaphysical escape from the problems of human existence, he attempted to discipline the mind. He recognized its powers, but he knew that it had to function in the province of life that experience apprehended. When, in "Ethan Brand," he invoked the ideal of understanding that proposes the human heart and the intellect in equipoise, he paid equal tribute to the dual expression of human nature in thought and feeling. He could not postulate a more valid philosophical reality.

The counterparts of our Biblical ancestors in "The New Adam and Eve" again reveal Hawthorne's attitude toward the existence and growth of evil in the universe. Possessing a full development of mind and heart in an uncorrupted state, the pair come to life in a world completely depopulated of its former inhabitants. Moving curiously about the streets and buildings of a perfectly preserved city of the old culture, Adam and Eve instinctively recognize purity and simplicity in taste, and are strongly attracted. Falseness and perversity, on the other hand, immediately repel them. In their respective reactions, Hawthorne sets up the familiar antithesis of the intellect and heart, of masculine and feminine qualities in exact balance. In this fashion he symbolizes an unsullied, primal morality. It is not long before Adam begins to speculate on "the interpretation of the riddles" amid which they wander."[51] The indecipherable print of a book that he has accidentally opened stimulates this goading train of thoughts. But with sound feminine instinct, Eve rescues him from the mysterious peril of the written word.

Hawthorne does not assume that Eve will forever thwart Adam's desire to understand himself and the world that surrounds him. This Faustian urge will, he realizes, never be suppressed. He does not, however, conjecture the reappearance of another Satan, who will feed them the fatal apple of a second Tree of Knowledge. Rather he presupposes that Adam will strive upward and onward, as will his progeny. Yet the path toward knowledge will be fraught with danger. Adam and his kin will often "fall short of good, even as far as we did; [they will have] at least the freedom — no worthless one — to make errors for [themselves]."[52] Thus, tacitly, Hawthorne repeats the thesis of "Ethan Brand": it is the unalterable condition of human existence that man will clear a path to truth and knowledge through the jungle of sin and sorrow.

Returning to his own times and reconsidering this irrepressible Faustian desire of man to know and to do, Hawthorne says in "Earth's Holocaust" that it is no more than an "endeavor for perfection," an attempt to realize the ideal that nature continually flaunts in the face of man. But the dilemma of man's Faustian nature, therefore the dilemma of the world in every phase of its development, is the inability to keep the balance of the intellect and the heart. This failing renders him liable to "the mockery of the evil principle," who declares that man will remain callous and evil until he "hit[s] upon some method of purifying that foul cavern [from which] will reissue all the shapes of wrong and misery. . . ."[53] This perfect reciprocity of the intellect and heart is Hawthorne's metaphor for the integration of personality. In psychological terms, to elaborate this idea further, he claims that the conscious ego must achieve a reconciliation with the desires of the unconscious for spiritual order and social stability. In a phrase, the individual will must condition itself to the tyranny of universal necessity which is transcendent. For, as in the case of Ethan Brand, when the mind, the conscious ego, asserts its right to unrestricted powers, the magnetic chain of humanity is broken, the great brotherhood of man becomes an illusion. Thus, in language as simple as a Christian parable, Hawthorne advocates a combined social and moral philosophy, an untheological religion of humanity. In the specific idiom of the mythic image or its ritual concomitant, the compact with the devil, experience with evil serves as the indoctrination into truth, that is, if self-awareness is the result. For knowledge of self symbolizes man's need to reconcile the outer world of physical nature, human action, and human endeavor with the inner world of his own conscious and unconscious responses to these things.

In arriving at this solution of the evil of his age, Hawthorne follows, though with admirable originality, the line of thought that gives Goethe's *Faust* its philosophical meaning. But whereas Goethe symbolically reflects the mode of his century's salvation in Faust's love for Gretchen, Hawthorne with greater clarity establishes the condition of mankind's salvation in the love of man for man. Evidence that Hawthorne was to attempt a further extension of his Faust myth is found in his various critical writings of this period. "P.'s Correspondence" and "A Select Party" divulge his continuing interest in the crucial devil-image. "Main Street" exhibits an ingenious "Faustiad" that reveals his skill in adapting the plastic motivations of the Faust myth, and "The Hall of Fantasy" shows him expressing an undisguised admiration for Goethe. Therefore when he draws the materials for his Faustian portraits from his meditations on contemporary life, he merely adds the colors and tints to his works that are inevitable as the method of his art deepens and improves.

And when he achieves his most meaningful characterization, in "Ethan Brand," the last completed of his five Fausts, it presages something greater. Aylmer, Rappaccini, Warland, and Drowne are, in an important sense, the preliminary models of Ethan Brand. In the lives of the others Hawthorne criticizes the external manifestations of the ideals of his age, visible in science and in a materialistic economy. In "Ethan Brand" he probes into the spiritual heart of his times, brushing away the thick clouds of abstract philosophy that hinder man's understanding of evil. "The New Adam and Eve" and "Earth's Holocaust" offer corroborative testimony that "Ethan Brand" was an effort to give good and evil a sensible value in terms of universal human experience. But the superlative achievement of Hawthorne was in the offing. In *The Scarlet Letter* he would realize the ambition to write the definitive New England *Faust*.

CHAPTER VIII

THE SCARLET LETTER: THE NEW ENGLAND *FAUST*

HE SCARLET LETTER is a Faustian synthesis that elaborates the spiritual enlightenment engendered by
experience with evil. The setting in early Puritan
times has both local and universal implications.
Standing aloof from the action, Hawthorne analyzes the intellectual
and spiritual aspirations of seventeenth-century New England in
terms of the clash of human conduct with the conventions of society. Thereby he is able to generalize universal truths from the
never-ending conflict of individual desire with community or tribal
taboos. To motivate the actions of his characters he relies upon
methods adapted from Faustian drama and from the Faustian-motivated Gothic novel. The three great dramatic versions of the Faust
myth — Marlowe's *Faustus,* Calderón's *Il Mágico Prodigioso,* and
Goethe's *Faust* — provide him with four traditional elements of the
pact with the Infernus: (1) a scholar (2) who practices magic (3)
places his soul in jeopardy, (4) though not without experiencing
a glimpse of ideal beauty.[1] And like the dramatists, Hawthorne
allows the historical background to determine the mode of salvation
or damnation. These standards particularly influence his characterization of Roger Chillingworth. The other main characters, Hester
Prynne, Arthur Dimmesdale, and Pearl, are modeled from their
Faustian prototypes in the Gothic romance.

Though the story ostensibly concerns itself with the effects of
sin upon the lives of these four characters, the dramatic movement
of the plot is controlled by the devil-archetype. The initial act of
adultery is the result of his intrigues. The subsequent behavior

of those persons either directly or indirectly affected by the sin is also inspired by the evil principle. This is the dramatic outline of of the plot. Those actions proscribed by society arise from the function of a supernatural agent of evil. But the resultant punishment is determined by the community. Two levels of reality are thus established: the historical and the natural.

In Goethe's *Faust* a similar phenomenon occurs. Mephistopheles is the motive power behind the other characters. The action into which he goads them always leads to their ruin, but without his stimulation it does not appear that there would be any action at all. Mephistopheles' role, though apparently that of a minor character, is really that of a prompter and stage-manager. He is a plotter who sets the conflict in motion and leads his puppets on to an assault on moral law that precipitates their doom.[2] In *The Scarlet Letter* Hawthorne ascribes Hester's silent rebellion against her punishment to the temptations of the fiend. Pearl's wildness is laid to supernatural causes. And Dimmesdale, after his meeting with Hester in the forest, acknowledges that he is infernally possessed. Chillingworth's metamorphosis into a tempter is the culmination of long service to the demon.

In the preface to *The Snow Image* Hawthorne suggests the two interpretations possible, on the natural and the historical levels of the romance. On the natural level, ". . . the purposes of psychological romance" determine his intention. This approach in *The Scarlet Letter* permits him to unravel the hidden relations of the four persons whose lives have been complicated by the sin of adultery. He merges this level with the historical, "arraying some of the ordinary facts of life in a slightly idealized and artistic guise."[3] This is a mythic technique, and in *The Scarlet Letter* the pact with the devil and the ritual archetype permit him to universalize the moral quandaries of the historical characters. Yet at no time does Hawthorne prescribe the proper mode of interpretation. Never betraying the complexity of his method of symbolization, he merely comments: "Every sentence, so far as it embodies thought or sensibility, may be understood and felt by anybody who will give himself the trouble to read it, and will take up [my works] in a proper mood."[4]

Though Hawthorne in *The Scarlet Letter* oscillates between these two levels, as skillfully enforcing the one as the other, the historical interpretation is generally considered more meaningful, and the natural, with its mythic imagery, is explained away, with uneasy grace, as a kind of inexplicable technical affectation. The indifference to Hawthorne's carefully differentiated order of form has resulted in an imperfect understanding of the novel, for it is in the penumbra of the supernatural, the mirror of the universal natural world, that the novel achieves its meaning. Correlated with the historical action the dramatic symbols of the Faust myth here operate with overwhelming import. The mocking demon, the emperor in this dark realm, tempts his victims into moral defections that endanger their souls. His visible emblem in the external world is the scarlet letter. It is the banner of evil waving over the moral territory that he has partly conquered.

This technique of interpretation makes the characters most important. Their reactions to the sin of adultery, the pre-narrative motivation, are the basis of Hawthorne's speculations on the problem of evil and on its associated intellectual and spiritual values. In the case of Chillingworth, who is usually treated as a piece of machinery, a new perspective on his function is afforded, removing the blight of insane jealousy which commonly destroys his real significance. Hawthorne logically motivates all of the physician's actions, and in his plunge to doom there is something of the pathos and tragedy that marked Ethan Brand. Chillingworth, it must be remembered, during most of his life dabbles in magical experiments that fall under the jurisdiction of the devil. Yet, unlike Ethan Brand, he is not impelled by the knowledge which he accumulates to break the magnetic chain of humanity; he continually keeps the welfare of mankind in sight. When he marries Hester, he hopes that she will inspire him to greater efforts. She represents his firmest tie to humanity; she epitomizes its sympathy, tenderness, and love. She links him to the deep heart of the universe. Having a profound faith in the integrity of Hester, he sends her to the New World, intending to follow her after he has arranged his affairs in Europe. Unfortunately, upon arrival he is captured and imprisoned by the Indians. After a lengthy incarceration he is ransomed, and immediately makes his way to the settlement where Hester resides. The first sight that greets his eyes is Hester on the pillory. In the terrible emotional distress that overcomes him, he sees his connection with the magnetic chain of humanity snapped. The grief which floods his heart drives him to a resolution that will, with inexorable finality, exile him from Hester's emotional world. He will, at the propitious moment, sell his soul to the devil, and proclaim his rejection of the brotherhood of man.

To emphasize Chillingworth's essentially heroic stature, Hawthorne sketches him as a Faust, whose prototype we encounter in the dramas. Hester's memories, as she stands on the scaffold, recapture one of her husband's Faustian traits. Her mind's eye dwells on "a pale, thin, scholar-like visage, with eyes dim and bleared by the lamplight that had served them to pore over many ponderous books. Yet those same bleared optics had a strange, penetrating power, when it was their owner's purpose to read the human soul."[5] In the prison-cell scene, as Chillingworth ministers to the ailments of Pearl and Hester, Hawthorne adds another Faustian quality to the scholar's character. Like all Fausts, he has found it necessary to pursue knowledge beyond ordinary limits; and, during his captivity with the Indians, he has learned the lore of medicine. Chillingworth, talking to Hester, leaves no doubt about his talents in this study: "My old studies in alchemy . . . and my sojourn . . . among a people well versed in the kindly properties of simples, have made a better physician of me than many that claim the medical degree."[6] Later Hawthorne imputes the old man's extraordinary skill to magic. An aged craftsman in the village declares that Chillingworth was once an associate of the notorious conjurer, Dr. Froman; and other individuals hint that he "had enlarged his medical attainments by joining in the incantations of the savage priests, who were universally acknowledged to be powerful enchanters, often performing seemingly miraculous cures by their skill in the black art." A vulgar rumor prevails that Chillingworth's dark and ugly face betrays his satanic connections. It is said that "the fire in his laboratory had been brought from the lower regions, and was fed with infernal fuel; and so, as might be expected, his visage was getting sooty with the smoke."[7]

At one point in the narrative Hawthorne makes a direct allusion to the scholar's Faustian antecedents: ". . . a rumor gained ground, — and, however absurd, was entertained by some very sensible people, — that Heaven had wrought an absolute miracle, by transporting an eminent Doctor of Physic, from a German university, bodily through the air, and setting him down at the door of Mr. Dimmesdale's study!"[8] Thus Hawthorne succeeds in endowing Chillingworth with the conventional traits of the familiar Fausts. Scholar, alchemist, magician, and physician, he resembles the Faustian hero who moves across the stage in the first scene of Marlowe's and Goethe's dramas.

Nor does Hawthorne fail to give Chillingworth a glimpse of ideal beauty. The disillusioned scholar confesses that the feelings Hester aroused defied rational definition, as they went beyond the ken of magical explanation: "It was my folly. . . . I, — a man of thought, — the book-worm of great libraries, — a man already in decay, having given my best years to feed the hungry dream of knowledge, — what had I to do with youth and beauty like thine own!"[9] Yet he concedes that she alone was able to give him a truly human status among his fellow men: ". . . up to that epoch of my life, I had lived in vain. The world had been so cheerless! My heart was a habitation large enough for many guests, but lonely and chill, and without a household fire. I longed to kindle one! It seemed not so wild a dream . . . that the simple bliss, which is scattered far and wide, for all mankind to gather up, might yet be mine."[10] This is the same ghost of beauty that Marlowe's Faustus invoked to ease the shock of disenchantment, the same one also that Goethe's aged Faust deemed a compensation for his failures. In the dream of perfect love they all could identify themselves with mankind.

It is this terrible sense of loss that prompts Chillingworth to

bargain away his soul to the devil. He will revenge himself on the
criminal who stole Hester's love. And when Hester will not disclose
her paramour's name, the old physician grimly asserts: "I shall seek
this man, as I have sought truth in books; as I have sought gold in
alchemy."[11] In other words, he will read the secret of guilt on her
betrayer's heart. But the sins that lie hidden in mortal bosoms are
not, as Ethan Brand discovered, for the eyes of prying mortals. On
Judgment Day they will be disclosed to God who will assign the
penalty the sinner must pay. But the Puritan Faust aspires for precisely this knowledge of secret evil. He will render justice in this
case. He will, as it were, usurp God's prerogative. His mind will
trespass into the forbidden portals of heaven. He will make a mockery of universal morality. He will deliberately disown his brotherhood with man and his reverence for God.

In effect, without a formal contract, Chillingworth consummates
a pact with Satan. Hawthorne, like Goethe, decrees the volition to
evil a sufficient condition of bondage. Yet no doubt is left that the
devil controls the will of the scholar-magician. After Hester refuses
to reveal the identity of her lover, the husband extorts a pledge of
silence from her on the legal state of their relations. But something
in his cruel smile causes her to regret her promise, and she inquires
in fear: "Art thou like the Black Man that haunts the forest round
about us? Hast thou enticed me into a bond that will prove the ruin
of my soul?" His answer is sardonically elusive: "Not thy soul!
No, not thine!"[12] Chillingworth, without as yet being sure of his
method, intends to plot against the soul of her unknown lover. The
Puritan Faust feels confident that his patience and diabolic art will
be rewarded in due time.

In this fashion Chillingworth aligns himself with the demon. He
enters into a covenant with the dark evils of his soul. He compromises the integrity of a long life dedicated to the improvement of
mankind. Just nine years before, he recalls, his life was "bestowed
faithfully for the increase of [his] own knowledge, and faithfully,
too, . . . for the advancement of human welfare. No life had been
more peaceful and innocent than [his]; few lives so rich with bene-

fits conferred."[13] As Hawthorne observes, Chillingworth at first deludes himself that he is the instrument of dispassionate justice. He attempts to rationalize his hate and jealousy as mere intellectual curiosity: "He had begun an investigation, as he imagined, . . . desirous only of truth, . . . as if the question involved no more than . . . a geometrical problem, instead of human passions, and wrongs inflicted on himself." But in a very short time his morbid interest in sin weakens his own resistance to it; his restrained emotions are transformed into a violent impulse of revenge: ". . . a terrible fascination, a kind of fierce, though still calm, necessity seized the old man within its gripe, and never set him free again until he had done all its bidding."[14] Thus Chillingworth commits spiritual suicide. He has as little control over his moral volition as did the Faust of the chapbook or Marlowe.

At this stage of Chillingworth's development at least three different Faustian variants have influenced Hawthorne's portrayal of the Puritan Faust. First, as in Reynold's *Faust*,[15] he uses the motive of revenge to implement a pact with the devil. Secondly, he skillfully applies Goethe's conception of informal bondage. And thirdly, the corruption of the moral will that informs both the chapbook and Marlowe's *Faustus* enters into his characterization of his magician. Having at the same time ascribed to the old physician those traits of the Fausts of the dramas and having expertly woven them into the pattern of action, Hawthorne has fabricated a Faust who is indigenous to the New England scene.

Hawthorne also introduces the theme of the elixir of life, so important in Goethe's *Faust,* into the complex delineation of Chillingworth. The implications of one reference to the elixir deepen the horror of the Puritan necromancer's insidious scheme of revenge. Hawthorne notes that the physician compounds the drugs and medicines used in treating Dimmesdale "as if the proposed result had been the Elixir of Life."[16] If not an elixir, these medicines do, as Chillingworth tells Hester, serve his purpose well: "But for my aid, his [Dimmesdale's] life would have burned away in torments. . . . Oh, I could reveal a goodly secret! But enough! What art can do,

I have exhausted on him. That he now breathes, and creeps about on earth, is owing all to me!"[17]

To intensify the spiritual degeneration that accompanies the growth of the maddened scholar's monomaniacal vindictiveness, Hawthorne resorts to external diabolic symbolism. In undertaking "a devil's office" the old man acquires the emblems of that office: "Ever and anon . . . there came a glare of red light out of his eyes; as if [his] . . . soul were on fire, and kept on smouldering duskily within his breast, until, by some casual puff of passion, it was blown into a momentary flame."[18] A further physical evidence of his moral degradation is visible as "the former aspect of an intellectual and studious man"[19] is gradually replaced by a look of fierce and searching ugliness. These outward alterations of his body do not go unnoted by his neighbors. They declare him to be a "diabolical agent [having] Divine permission, for a season, to burrow into the clergyman's intimacy, and plot against his soul."[20] Even Hester's daughter, little Pearl, warns her mother against the physician: "Come away, or yonder old Black Man will catch you! He hath got hold of the minister already. Come away, mother, or he will catch you!"[21] So far as Chillingworth himself is concerned, he admits his complete dedication to evil; he angrily tells a sympathetic Hester: "I have already told thee what I am! A fiend!"[22]

Hawthorne has a purpose in thus exhibiting the Puritan Faust's physical and spiritual deterioration. In this manner he forcefully and vividly shows the deficiency of an intellect that renounces the mediation of the conscience to pursue a futile course of revenge. Chillingworth is not an abstraction dictated by the expediency of the plot. Hawthorne wishes to evaluate the potential of wickedness lying dormant in minds that have divorced themselves from the accepted standards of ethical behavior. When the scientist or the scholar rejects the basic spiritual values which give life meaning, he invites the catastrophe of moral anarchy. Hawthorne, generalizing from Chillingworth's conduct, remarks that the outcome of such intellectual independence is an inhuman materialism: "In their researches into the human frame, it may be that the higher and more subtile faculties of such men were materialized, and that they lost the spiritual view of existence amid the intricacies of the wondrous mechanism, which seemed to involve art enough to comprise all of life within itself."[23] Chillingworth evinces this complete absorption in the methods of philosophical inquiry. The speculation encouraged by natural philosophy is to him a means to satisfy a diseased curiosity. In the presence of the town magistrates and the clergy he inadvertently challenges the moral interdictions of Puritan religious thought: He dares suggest philosophy as a means of discovering Pearl's father: "Would it be beyond a philosopher's research, think ye, gentlemen, to analyze the child's nature, and, from its make and mould, to give a shrewd guess at the father?"[24]

Hawthorne has still another effect to achieve in sustaining the illusion that Chillingworth is indeed a devil. Not only does the latter perform the function of fostering evil, but his external physical appearance is contrived to enhance his awesome appearance. In the supernatural shadow of *The Scarlet Letter* he is a tempter. He is so designated by Dimmesdale's parishioners, the minister himself, when he realizes his relations to the physician, brands him "tempter."[25] Yet Chillingworth is no ordinary demon of seductive evil. His antecedents reveal his close kinship to the Satan of the Puritan fathers. Aware of the efficacy of grace, Chillingworth wishes to forestall a public confession by Dimmesdale. If the minister, giving way to self-pity and moral cowardice, flees the settlement, then he will doom himself irrevocably to everlasting hell.

But notwithstanding the Puritan acuity of the tempter, his lineage is traceable to Goethe's Mephistopheles. His assault on the spiritual defenses of Dimmesdale is designed to lure the sinner away from God. This effort closely parallels the aim of Mephistopheles in the Prologue to *Faust*. Goethe's tempter announces to God that Faust will not be able to resist the enticements standing between him and service to the divine power. Faust, however, regaining his moral perspective in the last scene of Part One of the drama, rushes to the assistance of the girl whom he has reduced to a criminal. Thereby he eludes the toils of Mephisto. Dimmesdale, in refusing to succumb

to the attractive temptation of flight, similarly circumvents Chillingworth. With the Puritan necromancer's failure to prevent the minister's public confession, the final phase of his characterization is
attained. As in the other versions of the Faust myth, the historical
background of the action determines the ultimate fate of the hero.
Chillingworth's belief that he cannot pardon Dimmesdale's sin is
a projection of his utter moral collapse. Therefore he stoically
surrenders his soul to the devil. An unrepentant sinner, he thinks
himself the victim of divine predestination: "My old faith, long
forgotten, comes back to me, and explains all that we do, and all we
suffer."[26]

Hawthorne closely follows the dramatists, especially Goethe, in
creating the two aspects of Chillingworth's personality: the typical
Faust and the Mephistophelian tempter. His symbolic repertory,
however, has its parallels in the Faustian Gothic romance. Chillingworth's smouldering soul is kindled by a spark of association flying
from *Vathek*.[27] The piercing eye of Balzac's Melmoth reflects in
Chillingworth's infernal glare,[28] and Maturin's Melmoth echoes in
the transformation from a gifted scholar into a ruthless tempter.[29]
The increase in physical ugliness accompanying Chillingworth's
evil inclinations is almost identical with that of Hoffmann's Medardus.[30] Thus, with sure skill, Hawthorne achieves a symbolic synthesis of the Puritan Faust's spiritual devolution.

Hawthorne feminizes the Faust motif in depicting the character
of Hester Prynne. From the moment Hester commits her soul to
the cause of the devil, she ceases to be the standard heroine of the
typical romance, the shaping source of Hawthorne's inspiration.
Exiled from normal society and constantly attended by the demon,
she shows a remarkable development in intellect. In seven short
years she changes from an emotionally passionate girl into a dynamic
rebel against convention. And considering her Puritan antecedents,
her radical speculations are more iconoclastic than Chillingworth's.
She becomes, in other words, the feminine counterpart of Faust, a
virtual Puritan Fausta. Though Hester's adultery, a sin of passion,
partly links her with the devil's legions, it is not until she pledges

herself to silence regarding her connection with Chillingworth that she actually recognizes the authority of the evil principle. In the conspiracy of silence, she betrays an ulterior motive. She subconsciously asserts a wishful desire for earthly happiness with the man who contributed to her ruin. And unintentionally she becomes an accessory of Chillingworth in his scheme of revenge, undermining the minister's moral and physical life with her dream of illicit bliss. Hawthorne is quite explicit about her temptation:

It might be, too, — doubtless it was so, although she hid the secret from herself, and grew pale whenever it struggled out of her heart, like a serpent from its hole, — it might be that another feeling kept her within the scene and pathway that had been so fatal. There dwelt, there trode the feet of one with whom she deemed herself connected in a union. . . . Over and over again, the tempter of souls had thrust this idea upon Hester's contemplation, and laughed at the passionate and desperate joy with which she seized, and then strove to cast it from her. She barely looked the idea in the face, and hastened to bar it in its dungeon.[31]

Nor does she succeed in quelling the rebellion that rages in her heart and mind. Increasingly she questions the justice of her punishment. Behind the smug countenances of her persecutors, she sees intimations of evil worse than her own. In the embarrassment of certain members of her own sex, all supposedly earthly saints, she intuits secret sin. The fiend, "whose talisman was that fatal symbol," will leave her nothing to revere.[32] Her outward piety contradicts the general trend of her thoughts: "She assumed a freedom of speculation, then common enough on the other side of the Atlantic, but which our forefathers, had they known it, would have held to be a deadlier crime than that stigmatized by the scarlet letter."[33] She deplores the subordinate position of women in society, and believes that the system of masculine privilege, the double standard of ethics, ought "to be torn down, and built up anew."[34] As she gazes round her, she inwardly declares that "the world's law [is] no law for her mind.[35] This impatience with the conventions of the culture attests the Faustian tone of her meditations. Her intellectual curiosity savors of the sinful impulse that led her into adultery. She cannot "measure . . . ideas of right and wrong by any standard external to herself."[36] In all her thoughts she manifests the blind pride of Lucifer and his most notorious disciple, the ill-fated Faust.

This mental outlook serves to negate the Christian quality of her numerous acts of kindness in her role of "Sister of Mercy" in the Puritan settlement. On the surface, her benevolence and charity conform to the Calvinistic conception of penance. But in her heart, wherein only the love of God is supposed to dwell, an earthlier passion holds sway. Nothing, however, that she may think or do can change the tragic course of her life. Slowly despair overwhelms her, and she contemplates suicide: "At times, a fearful doubt strove to possess her soul, whether it were not better to send Pearl at once to heaven, and go herself to such futurity as Eternal Justice should provide."[37] Her distraught spiritual state has an analogue in Goethe's *Faust*. The hero ponders the problem of life's meaning and the futility of noble thoughts; then, melancholy and disillusioned, he discerns that suicide is the single phase of human destiny within his control. Neither his vast knowledge nor the wide range of his speculations encourages him to think that the conditions of human existence can be changed or are worth changing. He is a care-worn man who "sowed vanity to reap despair."[38] As he reviews the disappointments of the past and the hopelessness of the future, he dolefully concludes that all his struggles are self-deception: "Everything fails me — everything — these instruments mock me . . . in vain I call on science; I stand before the guarded door of nature."[39] This parallel scarcely seems a coincidence: it is another sum that rings out clearly on the register of associations spreading from Goethe's *Faust*. Only in this latter work does suicide emerge as a solution to the disquieting frustrations of thought and emotion.

When the pall shrouding Hester's spirit lifts, she resolves to take positive action. She arranges to meet the minister so as to tell him of the old physician's nefarious plan of revenge. At the same time she intends to advise him to take flight from the colony. Pearl, as if aware of her mother's desperate undertaking, demands information regarding her familiarity with the devil who haunts the "forest, and carries a book with him, — a big, heavy book, with iron clasps . . . this ugly Black Man offers his book and an iron pen to every-body that meets him here among the trees; and they . . . write their names with their own blood. And then he sets his mark on their bosoms! Didst thou ever meet the Black Man, mother?"[40] Hester thoughtfully considers the question, and then answers: "Once in my life I met the Black Man! This scarlet letter is his mark!"[41] This utterance is in direct contrast to the evasions which she had hitherto offered Pearl explaining her infamous emblem. Hester consciously admits her alliance with the devil; she is no longer interested in resisting the temptations of the demon who haunts her unconscious. Her interview with her former lover will represent an earnest effort to defy the laws of morality to which she has to date submitted, however reluctantly.

At this point Hawthorne changes Hester's role in the story to that of a tempter, the evolution of her character, in a sense, corres-ponding to Chillingworth's. Hawthorne depicts the manner in which she uses her powerful sexual attraction to govern Dimmes-dale's volition. The Faustian inspiration which controls Hawthorne's creative imagination stems from Lewis' *The Monk*. He takes pains to model Dimmesdale after Ambrosio, and to establish the Puritan divine's flaw of nature in his passionate animal drive. Like Am-brosio, Dimmesdale is held in high esteem by his parishioners, being thought "little less than a heaven-ordained apostle"[42] and "a mir-acle of holiness."[43] The pastor's outward piety and stern asceticism increase after his affair with Hester just as did Ambrosio's after his sexual debauches with Matilda. Dimmesdale's "devotion to study, his scrupulous fulfilment of parochial duty and . . . the fasts and vigils of which he made a frequent practice," become the wonder of his profession.[44] The strong sexual predisposition of the minister is shown in his proneness to anger, and Hawthorne comments that this was "the portion of him which the Devil claimed, and through which he sought to win the rest."[45] This is a parallel situation to *The Monk* which is almost beyond quibble.[46]

Identical motivations continue as the forest scene further develops. To lure Ambrosio into a pact with the devil, Matilda takes advantage of his sublimated lechery, and so Hester breaks down the inhibitions of Dimmesdale. When they are alone in the forest, she casts her scarlet letter aside; and when she lets her long hair flow loosely about her face, she recaptures the beauty which not too long before had made the minister forget his holy vows. As the divine responds to her devilish charms, she proposes that he seek his fortune across the seas, leaving no doubt that she will accompany him: "But thou shalt leave it all behind thee! It shall not cumber thy steps, as thou treadest along the forest-path. . . . Leave this wreck and ruin here where it hath happened. . . . There is happiness to be enjoyed!"[47] What greater temptation to the weakened morale of Dimmesdale could there be? This was a hope he had never dared to express. Thus when Hester convinces him that this is the only alternative to disgrace or death, she performs the duty of a tempter. Only his confession at the election ceremony, brought on by a knowledge of imminent death more than by his tortured conscience, prevents Hester from precipitating him into irretrievable damnation. Only years later does Hester sincerely repent. The minister frustrates her as much as he does Chillingworth.

Though Hawthorne portrays Dimmesdale's spiritual hypocrisy, he does not indicate that the minister is beyond redemption until the meeting in the forest. Dimmesdale has never renounced the teachings of the church, and he never forgets his holy mission: "Lost as my soul is, I would still do what I may for other human souls! . . . though an unfaithful sentinel, whose sure reward is death and dishonor, when his dreary watch shall come to an end!"[48] This resolution ceases to have meaning after Hester has relieved him of responsibility to his God. Hence he proceeds homeward, overflowing with exuberance and confidence. Hawthorne's observations on this transformation sharpen the perspective: "Before Mr. Dimmesdale reached home, his inner man gave him other evidences of a revolution in the sphere of thought and feeling. In truth, nothing short of a total change of dynasty and moral code, in that interior kingdom, was adequate to account for the impulses now communicated to the unfortunate and startled minister." How anarchic this moral revolution was is seen in his brief encounters with several of his admirers. Forced to engage a patriarch of the church in conversation, Dimmesdale has difficulty restraining "blasphemous suggestions . . . respecting the communion supper."[49] Similarly he has to exercise a strong self-control to keep from whsipering into the ear of a pious old lady an "unanswerable argument against the immortality of the human soul."[50] Though the impulse asserts itself again and again, he is fortunately able to maintain his clerical decorum. But suddenly he is struck by a thought that leaves him shuddering over the fate of his soul: ". . . am I given over utterly to the fiend? Did I make a contract with him in the forest, and sign it with my blood? And does he now summon me to its fulfilment, by suggesting the performance of every wickedness which his most foul imagination can conceive?" As if to dispel any doubt that he may have in his mind, Mistress Hibbins, a notorious witch, greets him familiarly. She immediately senses his dedication to the Infernus: "Without taking overmuch upon myself, my good word will go far towards gaining any strange gentleman a fair reception from yonder potentate you wot of![51] Hawthorne's psychological analysis of the minister's condition tends to illumine the cones of darkness in this supernatural projection: "The wretched minister! He had made a bargain very like it! Tempted by a dream of happiness, he had yielded himself, with deliberate choice, as he had never done before, to what he knew was deadly sin. And the infectious poison of that sin had been thus rapidly diffused throughout his moral system. It had stupefied all blessed impulses, and awakened into vivid life the whole brotherhood of bad ones."[52] This is ample evidence not only to confirm the minister's virtual contract with the devil, but also to clarify Hester's role in the original seduction. More importantly, however, Hawthorne's symbolic method is considerably simplified. He strives to communicate the reality of an experience on the spiritual level of existence by reference to a corresponding reality on the level of the supernatural. In the traditional symbolism of the Faust myth, he finds a valid correlative objective.

One symbolic detail, Dimmesdale's characteristic gesture of placing the hand over the heart, is explained by the stigma of the scarlet letter, which inexplicably appears on the minister's breast. But whether a mark of penance, or remorse, or necromancy, the motion excites the recollection of Beckford's *Vathek*. The identical gesture of Vathek signifies the extinction of moral goodness. Hawthorne, in borrowing the symbol, uses it to heighten the impression of Dimmesdale's agonizing feelings of guilt. And perhaps it is significant that the lure of happiness permitting an immediate escape from unbearable suffering is the temptation that both Balzac's and Maturin's Melmoth consider irresistible.[53]

The dramatic climax in the minister's characterization remains consistent with the spirit of the Faust tradition. As the suffering man proudly marches along the route of the election procession, Mistress Hibbins insinuates that the clergyman's reluctance to recognize the will of his infernal lord will be duly punished. She whispers this information to Hester: "When the Black Man sees one of his own servants, signed and sealed, so shy of owning to the bond as is the Reverend Mr. Dimmesdale, he hath a way of ordering matters so that the mark shall be disclosed in open daylight to the eyes of all the world!"[54] Even Hester admits that he hardly strikes her as the man she talked to in the forest. She fears that there is no "real bond betwixt the clergyman and herself."[55] In the hint of exposure to come and in the contrasting meanings of the bonds referred to by Mistress Hibbins and Hester, Hawthorne exemplifies his method of mingling the historical with the natural until they are almost indistinguishable. When, after the election sermon, Dimmesdale mounts the pillory in company with Hester and Pearl to confess his part in the adultery, his death "of triumphant ignominy before the people"[56] appears to assure him of salvation. His fate is resolved according to the traditional religious beliefs of the period embraced by the story, as is consistent with the Faustian pattern of the plot.

In a still more emphatic sense, the death-confession is a Faustian convention. It appears in the Faust chapbook, in Calderón, in Marlowe, and tacitly in Goethe.

In delineating the character of Pearl, Hawthorne fits her into his Faustian complex. She is, in the words of Mistress Hibbins, "of the lineage of the Prince of the Air,"[57] and it is this aspect of her nature that Hawthorne portrays in the evolution of his plot. Through illegitimate birth, Pearl is an outcast in the infantile world: "An imp of evil, emblem and product of sin, she had no right among christened infants."[58] This same belief prevails in Hester's mind. In designing the child's garb, she unconsciously models the clothes on the token that she wears upon her breast "to create an analogy between the object of her affection and the emblem of her guilt and torture."[59] Pearl's lawless deportment reflects the thoughts of her mother's rebellious mind. In effect, the child lives in Hester's moral world, and there Satan is emperor. Hester has unwittingly made her a servant to the principle of evil, and at times the guilty woman is shamed by the crime that she has perpetrated. In the mirror of Pearl's eyes, she often sees "a face, fiend-like, full of smiling malice, yet bearing the semblance of features that she has known full well, though seldom with a smile, and never with malice in them. It was as if an evil spirit possessed the child, and had just then peeped forth in mockery."[60] Pearl inherits all the enmity and passion of her mother's heart, as if by inalienable right. She is in constant conflict with the adverse world. The townspeople, seeking vainly to establish her paternity, can only conclude that Pearl's odd attributes are supernatural: "[They] had given out that poor little Pearl was a demon offspring; such as, ever since old Catholic times, had occasionally been seen on earth, through the agency of their mother's sin, and to promote some foul and wicked purpose."[61]

The isolation from the common moral world, being infernal in its origins, can only be terminated by a deed that will compensate for the sin of her birth. Psychologically, Pearl merely desires a recognition of her paternity. She intuitively senses that Dimmesdale is her father. Her restoration to the human community hinges on his willingness to confess this fact. Then she will be granted the total share of natural sympathies that are her birthright. Until she acquires them, she will remain an exile in the cold, emotional realm of her lonely thoughts. In Reynolds' *Faust* another child, similarly disoriented, is rescued from doom in a manner similar to Pearl's.[62] In the climactic scene of *The Scarlet Letter* Dimmesdale's confession, accomplished against the tempter's violent opposition, is the circumstance on which the salvation of both Pearl and her father pivots. Each is restored to one of the two orders into which thinking man divides the universe, she to the historical harmony of the human community and he to the natural-supernatural equipoise of the immortal realms.

On the basis of this analysis of *The Scarlet Letter* it appears that a fluid conception of the Faust myth is the dynamic principle of composition ruling Hawthorne's creative imagination. Motivating most of the action in the novel is a versatile Faustian devil whose repertory of tricks derives from the Faustian drama and the Faustian Gothic romance. As Hawthorne manipulates the controlling idea, he endows each of his main characters with an aim in life that falls into the pattern of universal human experience. His portrayal of Chillingworth as a Puritan Faust who is victimized by a hereditary interest in sin elevates the latter's fate to a plane of numbing pathos and tragedy. In depicting Hester as a Fausta, Hawthorne separates her from the ordinary romantic heroine accidentally entangled in a net of evil. Her desperate efforts as a Faustian tempter are designed to express the eternal philosophy of womanhood: consistent with her maternal instincts, a woman's destiny is linked firmly with her desire to attain happiness for herself, her children, and her mate. In terms of the variant of the Faust myth, assigning to Dimmesdale the character of a lascivious monk, Hawthorne, with poetic justice that betrays his true feelings about the minister, rewards the latter's ignominious spiritual hypocrisy and moral cowardice. And by recourse to another Faustian phenomenon, Hawthorne ennobles Pearl's struggle to achieve identity in the human family.

The dramatic device of archetypal ritual in the Faust myth, the selling of the soul to the devil, provides Hawthorne with an operational symbol that enables him to analyze vividly the spiritual quandaries of his actors. This symbol effectively enlarges the experiences of the characters beyond the historical theatre of Puritan times. Its associations embrace the whole complex of human desires that have given to man's life a deep significance and purpose. Hawthorne's Satan is not the principle of evil in Calvinistic theology; he is the dark fatality that eternally works in the affairs of humans who have trespassed into ethically uncharted domains of the intellect and the spirit. Only by conquering this evil which is compounded of the only two worlds man can know, the inner world of the soul and the outer of human activity, can the individual confront bravely the tragic discipline of his existence. With such implications underlying the structure of *The Scarlet Letter,* the novel assumes a greater importance than has hitherto been assigned to it in the history of American letters.

CHAPTER IX

THE NEW AMERICAN FAUST

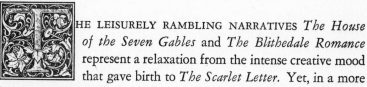

HE LEISURELY RAMBLING NARRATIVES *The House of the Seven Gables* and *The Blithedale Romance* represent a relaxation from the intense creative mood that gave birth to *The Scarlet Letter.* Yet, in a more important sense, they reflect a radical imaginative reorientation. From a rigid focus on the inner complexity of man's spiritual existence, Hawthorne's attention shifts to a consideration of the external values that shape and influence human conduct. By this change he announces a deliberate suppression of the tragic impulse of *The Scarlet Letter.* The visible pathos deriving from the frustration of human purpose now comes under his observation. With the same high seriousness that characterized his last novel he surveys the contesting aspirations evident in contemporaneous life. Discursive wisdom, mellowed by humor and irony, replaces the icy philosophical and psychological objectivity of the earlier works. He thus transforms tragedy into what might be termed moral romance. But as a consequence of this new artistic perspective, the ritual archetype of the Faust myth loses its organic function as a formula for tragedy. He converts the mythic devil-image and ritual process into static symbolic references.

In *The House of the Seven Gables* Maule's curse, as objectified in the seven-gabled mansion, is the Faustian symbol. It is the concrete manifestation of the Pyncheons' Faustian desire for wealth and power. It goads the first Pyncheon into evil as it does the last one. The symbol projects the different aspects of abnormal individual purpose in the successive generations of the family, and at the same time presents the different facets of evil that are at the center of uncontrollable egoistic desire.

Maule's curse also initiates the plot-movement, though immediately thereafter it relapses into the background of the unfolding action. In its origins the curse is a variant form of the ritual archetype of selling the soul to the devil. Colonel Pyncheon unwittingly allies himself with the satanic agent when he zealously urges the persecution of Matthew Maule for witchcraft in order to acquire the latter's property. On the scaffold Maule pronounces an eternal curse on the Puritan magistrate and his progeny. The efficacy of this curse is recognized when the Colonel dies on the day that he dedicates the mansion built on the dead man's property. Since the huge house was to symbolize Pyncheon's ascent to great renown in the form of a vast grant of territory in the state of Maine, the devil collects his due at this critical moment. With the old man's death, the secret location of the deeds to the Maine estate is lost. Thenceforth his offspring come under the spell of the curse by seeking these documents whose hiding place is known only to the Maules, one of whom was the architect of the house of the seven gables. By the first Maule's necromantic power, all the Pyncheons are rendered "no better than bond-servants to [the] plebeian Maules. . . ."[1] Thus Colonel Pyncheon's pride, which led him to meddle with justice, is fittingly rewarded. As Hawthorne notes, the witch trials "proved far less acceptable to the Beneficent Father than to that Arch Enemy whom they were intended to distress and utterly overwhelm."[2]

The evil nature of the ambition that incited the Colonel to tamper with the natural processes of the law asserts itself again in his grandson. Eager to obtain the Maule lands so as to buy himself a royal title, Gervayse Pyncheon permits a Maule to mesmerize his daughter. The only outcome of the feat is to place Alice Pyncheon's will power forever under the control of Matthew Maule. In this manner Gervayse loses salvation by selling his daughter "for the mere hope of getting a sheet of yellow parchment into [his] clutch."[3]

In the main body of the romance Judge Pyncheon is "tempted by

the devil"[4] into an act that involves the death of his uncle, the ille-
gal destruction of the will, and a trumped-up murder charge against
his cousin, the real heir. This chain of villainy springs from his
desire to attain ownership of the house of the seven gables. Ultimately this eagerness to find the papers proving his rights over the
Maine property results in his death. "Maule's curse," deftly symbolized by the ritual contract with the devil, is the fatal blow crush-
ing the Judge as the achievement of his career is in the offing, the
governorship of the state.

Though this Faustian symbol precipitates the action of *The House
of the Seven Gables,* Hawthorne does not allow it to intrude upon
his chief narrative considerations: the pathetic struggles of Hepzi-
bah and Clifford and the love story of Phoebe and Holgrave. Only
in the opening chapter and in the interior story of Alice Pyncheon
is the symbol in the foreground as the index of evil ambition. This
plot, indirectly stemming from Judge Pyncheon's overweening aspirations, provides Hawthorne with numerous pegs upon which he
can hang his social and political criticism. He shows no willingness
to darken these observations with the deeper implications of his
pivotal imagistic references. Having given them an external function at the beginning of his tale, he does not change their operative
values.

Hawthorne, however, does on occasion resort to the use of the
minor symbols proliferated by his mythic method. Judge Pyncheon
betrays his satanic relations by a familiar physical emblem, as did
Roger Chillingworth. In moments of infernal anger "a red fire [is]
kindled in his eyes . . . with something inexpressibly fierce and
grim darkening forth. . . ."[5] In another instance Hawthorne utilizes the device of the enchanted mirror to enhance the supernatural
significance of the Maule influence. The posterity of Maule have a
connection with the mystery of the looking glass in the Pyncheon
mansion; they, in sardonic whimsy, "make its inner region all alive
with the departed Pyncheons; not as they had shown themselves to
the world nor in their better and happier hours, but as doing over
again some deed of sin, or in the crisis of life's bitterest sorrow."[6]

On another occasion Hawthorne invents a symbol to indicate the moral degeneracy of the Pyncheons. A dwarfed breed of chickens that feed in the yard "betokened the oddities of the Pyncheon family, . . ."[7] their sterile isolation from community ideals. But in accordance with the loose character of the story Hawthorne keeps to a minimum his Faustian symbolism.

In *The Blithedale Romance* he again uses conventional Faustian imagery to impart an air of wonder to his romance. But as in the former novel it is not pervasive. To emphasize the wickedness that he believes inherent in theories of reform and in mesmerism, he resorts to the devil-archetype. He attributes Hollingsworth's obsession with philanthropic reform to a formidable egotism, which the latter mistakes for the inspiration of an angel of God. The reformer's scheme of benevolence is so narrow that it cannot tolerate other methods of charitable planning. Hollingsworth's purpose in life has so inverted his ethical values that he is incapable of sympathy and love unless they are related to his project. He worships an image of himself which the fiend has implanted in his mind. He would sacrifice "whatever is most precious; and never once seem to suspect — so cunning has the Devil been . . . that" his ideal "is but a spectrum of" himself "projected upon the surrounding darkness."[8] His complete subjection to inner evil is illustrated in the words of one of his innocent victims, whose happiness he sacrifices to the success of his scheme: "The fiend, I doubt not, has made his choicest mirth of you these seven years past, and especially in the mad summer which we have spent together. I see it now!"[9] In a final judgment Hawthorne describes the monomaniacal reformer as the "steel engine of the Devil's contrivance, a philanthropist!"[10] This method of juxtaposing ethical perversion with implied bondage to the devil demonstrates the effectiveness of Hawthorne's static mythic symbolism.

The other villain of the piece, Westervelt, is perfectly contrived to integrate with Hawthorne's allusions to *diablerie*. A professional mesmerist, Westervelt has an occupation similar to the devil's: the imposition of his will upon other beings. Hawthorne depicts his relations with Zenobia as extremely sinister, and Priscilla is the hypnotist's most responsive medium. Under Westervelt's cunning suggestions Priscilla displays a gift of second sight and prophecy. So astounding are these revelations that people "averred that the strange gentleman was a wizard, and that he had taken advantage of Priscilla's lack of earthly substance to subject her to himself, as his familiar spirit, through whose medium he gained cognizance of whatever happened, in regions near or remote."[11] Hawthorne also declares that "every human being, when given over to the Devil, is sure to have the wizard mark upon him, in one form or another."[12] Westervelt takes no pains to conceal his. Not only does he carry the symbolic cane of the fiend, "a stick with a wooden head, carved in vivid imitation of that of a serpent,"[13] but his smile reveals upon his upper teeth a border of gold that is "the Devil's signet."[14] This obvious sign of the devil is enough to suggest that the mesmerist is a "goblin" masquerading in the guise of a young man who "with all his show of manly beauty, [is] really an aged and wizened figure, or else that his semblance of a human body [is] only a necromantic, or perhaps a mechanical contrivance, in which a demon walked about."[15] When Zenobia refers to Westervelt, she designates her nemesis as a magician who "was the handsomest man in the world," and who "had bartered his own soul for seven years' possession of a familiar fiend. . . ."[16] It is interesting to note that the seven years is precisely the period of time that Zenobia declares to be the duration of her subjection to Hollingsworth, the other disciple of the fiend.

Coverdale's impression of Westervelt confirms the general opinions of the other characters. He looks upon the mesmerist as a Mephistophelian tempter, the epitome of the spirit of denial. After a short conversation with the wizard-marked gentleman, Coverdale is inclined to cynicism. Westervelt's criticisms of Hollingsworth, Zenobia, and Priscilla leave the young writer without faith in humanity. He begins to doubt all life's lofty ideals. His mood of disbelief leads him to disparage the moral beauty of heroism, and he wonders if it is not folly to attempt to benefit the world. Under the

influence of the pseudo-scientist's "cold skepticism,"[17] Coverdale
is moved to question the sincerity of all his friends.

Hawthorne himself implies that even Zenobia's suicide is explain-
able in her desire to escape the diabolic toils of the wizard. While
dredging the lake for her body, Coverdale and his companions believe their efforts retarded by an invisible force, "the Evil One, on the
same errand as [themselves], — searching for Zenobia."[18] When
they finally pull her body out of its watery grave, there is evidence
that she died engaged in a desperate struggle with her relentless
foe. Her fists are "clenched in immitigable defiance."[19] At her
funeral, which the mesmerist attends, he looks upon the ceremonies
gloomily but without actual grief. When Coverdale denounces him
as Zenobia's evil fate, he coldly remarks: "She is now beyond my
reach. Had she lived, and hearkened to my counsels, we might have
served each other well."[20] On this richly allusive Faustian note
Hawthorne concludes the major action of *The Blithedale Romance.*

But in addition there are scattered throughout the novel scin-
tillating scraps of poetic fancy and philosophical reverie, all vivi-
fied by Faustian lore. While lying abed in the uncomfortable sur-
roundings of the Blithedale farm, Coverdale wistfully muses on
the convenience of his apartment in the city. In an item of magian
skill first popularized in the Faust chapbook, his imagination finds
the association to heighten the contrast: "[There] where I had a
hundred dishes at command, and could banquet as delicately as the
wizard Michael Scott when the Devil fed him from the king of
France's kitchen."[21] And then his mind is swayed by memories of
demonic ritual: ". . . a horned and long-tailed gentleman (in
whom I recognized the fiendish musician erst seen by Tam O'Shan-
ter) tuned his fiddle, and summoned the whole motley rout to a
dance. . . . So they joined hands in a circle, whirling round so
swiftly, so madly, and so merrily, in time and tune with the Satanic
music. . . ."[22] Pondering the strange fortunes of Zenobia and Priscilla, he digresses to topical variations of the nucleating mythic ritual: "I saw . . . in Zenobia, the sorceress herself . . . fair enough
to tempt Satan with a force reciprocal to his own; and, in Priscilla,

the pale victim, whose soul and body had been wasted by her spells."[23] In this whimsical fashion Hawthorne's imagination remains thrall to the Faust myth.

Thus *The House of the Seven Gables* and *The Blithedale Romance,* though devoted to a serious inquiry into the various modes of contemporary thought, exhibit aspects of the Faust myth which are reconcilable with the essentially romantic nature of the plots. The melodramatic death of Judge Pyncheon and the suicide of Zenobia do not capture the spirit of tragedy; the incidents are anticlimactic, effecting no tragic purgation. Hawthorne merely reports the external manifestations of spiritual distress, or he ignores them entirely. The overt acts of his characters, in terms of their relation to ethical truth, are his main concern. And wherever he sees evil in performance, he equates it with diabolic activity. Whether it be Maule's curse, Hollingsworth's fiendish egotism, or Westervelt's wizard-inspired mesmerism, he first gives the motivation a moral location in the geography of the Faust myth, specifically in the ritual bargain with the devil. Thereafter this ethical judgment subsumes the larger narrative pattern of the story. Having once established his symbolic reference, he found no need to elaborate its meaning any further.

In Hawthorne's last completed novel, *The Marble Faun,* the elements of his archetypal imagery are again subordinated to the larger theme of the novel: the educative effects of sin. But as in the two romances that immediately followed *The Scarlet Letter,* he still insists upon tying up the original impulse toward sin with a variation of the pact with the devil. In this instance the specter of the catacombs functions as a Mephistopheles. This sinister figure, who is described "as personating the demon's part in a picture of more than two centuries ago,"[24] appears before Miriam as mysteriously as if magically invoked. Out of the shadows of the tunneled labyrinth beneath the city of Rome, he emerges to declare: "Henceforth, I am nothing but a shadow behind her footsteps. She came to me when I sought her not. She has called me forth, and must abide the consequences of my reappearance in the world."[25]

Though he becomes Miriam's model, he is alleged to be a demon who "has haunted the wide and dreary precincts of the catacomb, seeking . . . to beguile new victims into his own misery . . . endeavoring to prevail on any unwary visitor to take him by the hand, and guide him out into the daylight." Miriam, "with a strange air of seriousness over all of her face,"[26] confesses that she has entered into a pact with one of the disciples of Satan:

> . . . meeting the old infidel in one of the dismal passages of the catacomb, she had entered into controversy with him, hoping to achieve the glory and satisfaction of converting him to the Christian faith. For the sake of so excellent a result, she had even staked her own salvation against his, binding herself to accompany him back into his penal gloom, if, within twelve-months' space, she should not have convinced him of the errors through which he had so long groped and stumbled. But, alas! up to the present time, the controversy had gone direfully in favor of the man-demon.[27]

By this method Hawthorne sets up the ritual symbolic reference of the pact with the devil. Nor does he neglect to enforce this idea up until the time that Miriam and Donatello are lured into crime; but thereafter the motivation ceases to operate. He is more interested in the ordeal of sin and its influence on the attainment of spiritual truth.

Hawthorne reports a conversation between Miriam and the demon to verify further her strange bondage. The diabolical shadow urges upon her a way of life that is consistent with his mission of evil in the universe: ". . . there remains so much to be sinned and suffered in the world. We have a destiny which we must needs fulfil together."[28] When Miriam demurs, he threatens her with the most intolerable disgrace: "You know the power that I have over you. Obey my bidding; or, within a short time, it shall be exercised: nor will I cease to haunt you till the moment comes."[29] And at one time on the public street Miriam is glimpsed "kneeling to this dark follower there in the world's face!"[30] Hawthorne in these varied ways openly strives to create the impression that Miriam is the slave of the demon of the catacombs.

As Hawthorne expands the details of this relationship, he increasingly molds the model as the adversary of God. The canny protagonist of evil insidiously suggests murder to Miriam as her only mode of escape from his persecution. If she will not yield to his invitations to evil, then he will tempt her into an act that will damn her with finality. Exactly as the tempter foresaw, Miriam cannot gainsay the efficient weapon of murder. Standing with Donatello on the heights overlooking Rome one evening, she tells her lover that, in days gone by, the Romans used to cast all criminals to their death from this spot: "Men whose lives were the bane of their fellow-creatures, . . . who poisoned the air, which is the common breath of all, for their own selfish purposes. There was short work with such men in old Roman times."[31] At this psychological moment the model, who has been following the couple, detaches himself from the shadows behind them, and moves toward Miriam. Donatello, acting under the impulse of the story and the flash of assent in Miriam's eyes, heaves the fiendish persecutor to his death on the rocks below. Thus the man-demon had enticed not one but two persons into an act that would deprive them of salvation. Having motivated the commission of sin through an ingenious adaptation of the archetypal covenant, Hawthorne now gets on with the main purpose of the story: to write the epic of the soul's growth.

This larger theme of the novel merits some discussion, for there is a possibility that Hawthorne here is developing in narrative form the implications of Goethe's *Faust*. Accepting, as does Goethe, the probability that evil is destined to overcome man in his odyssey through life, Hawthorne presents the experience of Donatello and Miriam as the typical evolution of the human soul which foreshadows the destiny of all mankind. In short, ethical truth comes to the individual, not in passive meditation secluded from life's indiscriminate assaults on the soul, but in mortal struggle with the infernal desires that ever tempt the imperfect human being. In the recurring conflict between good and evil, which no one can avoid, the soul, according to its quality, either recoils from the shock of its depraved inclinations or courageously admits its radical flaws. In this latter condition the spirit of man may temporarily assume that it has fallen into the bottomless abyss of hell, but, possessing a volition toward virtue, it may rise again to confront the burning light of truth with steady eyes. Tempered by guilt and pain as fierce as purgatorial flame, the spiritual nature of man asserts its ability to cope with the dark tragedies that are inevitable in earthly existence. This conclusion issues from both *The Marble Faun* and *Faust*.

Casting his ominous shadow over one segment of this ordeal of sin is a demon who is a counterpart of Goethe's spirit of negation. The scornful voice of this fiend is heard by Hilda, whose rigid moral principles are invulnerable: "[She] now grew acquainted with that icy demon of weariness, who haunts great picture galleries. He is a . . . Mephistopheles. . . . He annihilates color, warmth, and, more especially, sentiment and passion, at a touch."[32] This gallery-Mephistopheles also affects Hilda's friendship with Miriam. The New England maiden is unable to sympathize with Miriam's misfortune. She declares that the latter's deed "has darkened the whole city."[33] Hilda refuses to acknowledge the possibility that right and wrong, "two things so totally unlike[,] can be mistaken for one another" or that "Right and Wrong . . . can work together in the same deed."[34] Therefore the innocent girl severs her friendship with the unhappy criminal. Hawthorne implies that Hilda is deluded by the sophisms of self-righteousness. Her intolerance springs from the demon in her own mind who whispers that her moral life is sacrosanct. Hawthorne scores her narrow perspective on the moral life, her reluctance to extend her sympathies beyond herself. The Mephistopheles who destroyed her warm and tender sympathies for great art bestows his curse upon her spiritual integrity.

Though the ritual act of evil that is inseparable from the devil-image does not enter into all of *The Marble Faun,* it nevertheless provides the motivation which activates the movement of the main plot. Miriam's bondage to the specter of the catacombs, which Hawthorne aligns with a covenant, leads directly to the crime of Donatello and Miriam, which becomes the core of the novel and the

subject of Hawthorne's speculations on the educative role of sin in
human life. This theme bears some resemblance to Goethe's formulation of Faust's predicament in the Prologue to Part One of *Faust*.
Certainly Hawthorne was not unaware that Goethe expressed a
viewpoint similar to his. And in Hilda's susceptibility to Mephistophelian denial lies a logical explanation of her Puritan intolerance, one of the ramifications of Hawthorne's Faust myth in the
earliest period of his writing. But as in *The House of the Seven
Gables* and *The Blithedale Romance,* Hawthorne in this novel
colors only the fringes of the plot with the brilliant dyes of his
archetypal imagery.

Hawthorne's unfinished romances,[35] all of which are different
developments of the same germinal themes, suggest that at the end
of his life he determined once again to write a Faustian tragedy.
The first study for the new tale, *The Ancestral Footstep,* is based
upon the plot of an Englishman who migrates to America carrying
away with him a family secret that will give his descendants the
power to ruin the persons residing in the mother country. Inte-
grated with this motivation is the legend of the bloody footstep
which is imprinted on the threshold stone of the ancestral mansion.
In this narrative there is no hint, however, that the story will take
a Faustian turn. When Hawthorne re-introduces these two themes
into *Doctor Grimshawe's Secret,* he modifies them with ideas deriving from the mythic images of the Faust story. Attempting to sketch
one of his major characters, Doctor Grimshawe, he decides that "a
certain grim atmosphere of mystery" must be evoked: "It [is] well
to present him to the readers as seen through the observations and
conjectures of an imaginative boy. He shall also practice experiments in natural science and shall have a tradition of medical knowledge from having been originally intended for a doctor."[36] The
associations operating in this statement need no comment: the
Faustian lineaments of Doctor Grimshawe are self-evident.

To symbolize the Doctor's wickedness Hawthorne next settles on
a huge tropical spider. He states that the ugly monster is the old
man's demon, and therein lies a revelation. The Doctor, who has

under his guardianship two children, Ned and Elsie, is portrayed as
a gruff and sardonic figure with a habit of mocking his little charges.
On those occasions when his better nature stoops to moral instruc-
tion, the influence of the spider is immediately exercised. The insect, by a few significant movements, signifies its displeasure with
the apothecary, and thereupon the old man tries "to turn the whole
matter into jest": "Crusty Hannah [the housekeeper], who [is]
drawn to the door of the study by the unusual tones of his voice
. . . always averred that she saw the gigantic spider swooping
round his head in great crafty circles, and clutching, as it were, at his
brain with its great claws. But it was the old woman's absurd idea
that this hideous insect was the Devil, in that ugly guise. . . ."[37]
As Hawthorne contrives this situation, there is no difficulty in tracing the source of the inspiration. In the body of the spider is imprisoned the spirit of the Mephistophelian demon that darkened so
many other narratives. The familiar of Doctor Grimshawe, he tol-
erates no digressions into virtue by his bond slave. Disdain and
ridicule are permitted — nothing else.

Hawthorne firmly establishes Doctor Grimshawe's connection
with the English emigrant of *The Ancestral Footstep.* He also explains the old man's desire to warp the mind of Ned through a plan
whereby he will make the boy the instrument of his revenge on the
family in England. The Doctor himself links his plot to an infernal
pact: ". . . supposing I had a darling purpose, to the accomplishment of which I had given my soul, — yes, my soul, — my success
in life, my days and nights of thought . . . pledging myself to it,
until at last I had grown to love the burden of it, and not to regret
my own degradation." And musing on this statement, he concludes
that the force shaping his will must bring things "to a sudden end-
ing."[38] Quite clearly he admits that the devil will, sooner or later,
collect his due. Like the vindictive diabolism of Chillingworth in
The Scarlet Letter, he too betrays his satanic character by physical
manisfestations. His countenance is contorted into hideous grimaces
that denote the constrictive hand of the devil on his soul: "if you
looked in his face, there was the red, lurid glare of his eyes; meeting

you fiercely and craftily as ever: sometimes he bit his lip and frowned in an awful manner."[39]

Other evidence is offered that the fiend is the malevolent power that shapes the destiny of Ned in his adult years. The young man unknowingly becomes the agent of the Doctor's revenge when he lays claim to an ancestral mansion in England. The large house becomes a symbol of an evil similar to that represented in *The House of the Seven Gables:* "It seemed as if the estate were possessed by a devil, — a foul and melancholy fiend, — who resented the attempted possession of others by subjecting them to himself."[40] Once Ned gains admission to the castle, the attraction of the place becomes irresistible. The active principle of ambition, which has been the touchstone of his life, asserts itself strongly. He shudderingly acknowledges to himself that the old forces of evil are at work: ". . . the witchcraft of the place was really to be recognized, the old witchcraft, too, of the Doctor. . . ."[41] This conviction is strengthened when he sees the hideously swollen spider which had been Grimshawe's familiar. Ned fancies that all "the poison of old times condensed into this animal, who might have sucked the diseases, moral and physical, of all this family into him, and to have made himself their demon."[42] The hereditary fiend of the family, he had tempted each of them with a prize of superiority and nobility, discerning with cold, malicious eye the Faustian ambitions that curdled their kindlier emotions. Now the spider-devil watches the American into whom old Doctor Grimshawe had injected the fatal germ of an implacable longing for fame.

Hawthorne was not satisfied with the story as he had outlined it. Apparently it failed to live up to the expectation of the major production that he had projected, the work in which he "ambitiously proposed to convey more of various modes of truth"[43] than he had ever before in his writings. Hence he abandoned the project. But immediately he began to plan another romance, *Septimius Felton,* with a theme of immortality. When published, the tale stimulated a piece of criticism especially important to this study. T. W. Higginson described the work as a masterpiece. He contended that it bore comparison with Goethe's *Faust,* and offered an elaborate interpretation of its meaning.[44] Later Lathrop repeated Higginson's opinion, also suggesting that Septimius Felton is "Faust at an earlier stage of development than that in which Goethe represents him."[45]

An analysis of the various manuscript versions of *Septimius Felton* supports the judgments of both Higginson and Lathrop. The recently uncovered studies reveal Hawthorne musing on the type of individual Septimius should be. The ambitions or ideals that would incite him to desire earthly mortality are considered. Details of action are explored. In one of the last studies Hawthorne indicates that his imagination is gravitating toward a Faustian definition of motive. The notes scribbled on the manuscript pages are very revealing; for, in one instance, he gives a tragic summary of the pact with the devil which, even with its Puritan associations, captures the distinctive spirit of the Faust myth: "Traditions of the temptation — the Divine used to have to go into the Forest and meet the Devil, and his wizard ancestor, and how his whole life was a struggle thereby, and his death troubled."[46] Though Hawthorne mentions traditions of the temptation, his outline embraces the general circumstances of Faust's life and death. Further on in the same study, Hawthorne adapts the idea to Septimius' forebears. One of them "becomes chief of a tribe of Indians, a great medicine man, or prophet and priest; when the Puritans come, they find him in this position, and consider him a wizard."[47] Of course, to be noted in these jottings are innumerable parallels that went into the characterization of Hawthorne's other magnificent Faust, Roger Chillingworth.

In the marginalia of a long scenario Hawthorne's figure of a Faust begins to crystallize. He models him after Goethe's Faust, assigning to his heroine a role similar to Gretchen: "Septimius must be endowed with grand and heroic qualities; and must desire a long life, not meanly, but for noble ends. No mean dread of death, but an abhorrence of it, as being childish, inactive, unsuitable. Make his nobility grow upon the reader, in spite of all his defects. It shall be on this occasion, too, that Sybil finally loves him, and spares him, and sacrifices herself instead." Hawthorne specifies a wonderful project to be envisioned by Septimius, one not unlike Faust's in Part Two of Goethe's drama: "One of Septimius's grand objects is to reform the world . . . if he can only live long enough to understand the nature of man." So far as Hawthorne formulates a philosophical truth to be illustrated in his Faust's experience, it is merely tentative: "the folly of man thinking that he can ever be of any importance to the world."[48] And like the Faust of Goethe, he will be visited by periods of despondency regarding his pursuits, imagining them to be "utter folly and impracti[ca]bility."[49]

Before examining one of the completed drafts of *Septimius Felton,* we must recall that the romance was never brought to the point of development which the author considered adequate enough to merit publication. But even in the abortive state, the work provides illuminating glimpses into an imagination that never could restrain its early dedication to the fascinating themes of the Faust myth, especially in their relation to the meaning of evil and the nature of spiritual truth.

The character sketched by Hawthorne in the opening scenes of the story stands at the crossroads of destiny. Septimius' knowledge persistently leads him into blind alleys. The secrets of nature defy his intelligence: ". . . with his head bent down, brooding, brooding, his eyes fixed on some chip, some stone, some common plant . . . as if it were the clue and index to some mystery . . . when, by chance startled out of these meditations, he lifted his eyes, there would be a kind of perplexity, a dissatisfied, foiled look in them, as if of his speculations he found no end."[50] The prototype of Hawthorne's frustrated scholar is of course Goethe's Faust, who, in the soliloquy in his study, laments that he stands "before the guarded door of nature."[51] Despairing of any attainment in the brief span allotted to man, Septimius gloomily ponders the vanity of existence. His little knowledge proves the impossibility of acquiring the vast amount that he desires. Time remorselessly mocks his petty endeavors: ". . . so much trouble of preparation to live, and then no life at all; a ponderous beginning, and nothing more."[52] A

similarly constructed situation is found in Goethe. The scholar
gives assent to Wagner's observation on the fleeting nature of life.
There remains no human solution to the problem, for death cannot be circumvented:

> *Oh! with what difficulty are the means*
> *Acquired, that lead us to the springs of knowledge!*
> *And when the path is found, ere we have trod*
> *Half the long way — poor wretches! we must die!*[53]

As Septimius sits in his library scanning the huge volumes containing the profoundest knowledge of men, he is overcome by the
futility of other men's thoughts: "Then he began to see that there
must have been some principle of life left out of the book, so that
these gathered thoughts lacked something that had given them their
only value. Then he suspected that the way truly to live and answer
the purposes of life was not to gather up thoughts into books, where
they grew so dry, but to live . . . not in maxims cut and dry, but
a wisdom ready for daily occasions. . . ."[54] An identical discon-
tent plagued Faust:

> *A mass of things confusedly heaped together;*
> *A lumber-room of dusty documents,*
> *Furnished with all-approved court-precedents,*
> *And old traditional maxims! History!*
> *Facts dramatized say rather — action — plot —*
> *. . . with many a moral apophthegm,*
> *And wise old saws, learned at the puppet shows.*[55]

There seems no need to elaborate Hawthorne's indebtedness to Goethe in the depiction of Septimius. His object is, as in the source, to
create a deep conviction of the limitations of man's knowledge in
the mind of his character. His next step is to transform this feeling
into a hatred of knowledge, so as to justify the recourse to magic.
Hawthorne does not detail the Faustian ritual of conjuration. The
devil is symbolized in the document which holds the secret of the
elixir of life. Hawthorne attributes the power of demonic invocation

to the ciphered manuscript, for as Septimius pores over the inscrutable sentences, he begins to believe that he will "succeed in reading" it only "if it might summon up a subject-fiend, appearing with thunder and devilish demonstrations."[56]

Hawthorne conceives of Septimius as the victim of a Mephistophelian demon, a spirit of denial: "doubts . . . strange, disheartening suggestions of the Devil, that so surely infect certain temperaments . . . were tormenting poor Septimius, and pulling him back from the path in which he was capable of doing so much good."[57] And it is not long before Septimius' mind is permeated by all these negations. He anathematizes the providence frustrating man's ambitious quests: "We are the playthings and fools of Nature, which she amuses herself with during our little lifetime, and then breaks for mere sport, and laughs in our faces as she does so."[58] And gradually his dabbling in magic forces him into a domain of ethical reality centered in his own ego: ". . . he felt that the solitary pursuit in which he was engaged carried him apart from the sympathy [of others] . . . his final triumph would be the complete seclusion of himself from all that breathed, — the converting him, from an interested actor into a cold and disconnected spectator of all mankind's warm and sympathetic life."[59]

Ultimately, following in the steps of Goethe's Faust, the young man's indifference to conventional morality leads to murder. On an occasion of Aunt Keziah's illness, he decides to dose her with his elixir. A short time after she drinks the draught, she dies. His only emotion regarding her demise is an urgent curiosity to know whether his mixture was responsible. He feels no remorse. His attitude is one of disinterested scientific wonder: "Something must be risked in the cause of science. . . . Septimius, much as he loved life, would not have hesitated to put his own life to the same risk that he had imposed on Keziah. . . ."[60]

Thus Hawthorne succeeds in bringing Septimius to a stage of moral degradation similar to that of Faust at the time when he is indirectly responsible for the death of Gretchen's mother and brother. But from this point on, Hawthorne relies upon his own inven-

tive genius. Holding to his original intention of planting the roots
of his plot deep in New England soil, he now relates Septimius'
experiments to the influence of the Black Man. And in this interval
the New England Faust's achievements are rumored to be of an
extraordinary dimension, and "the Black Man" is said to have "met
him on the hill-top, and promised him an immediate release from
his difficulties, provided he would kneel down and worship him,
and sign his name in his book. . . ."[61] Yet this young Faust fails
to decoct the elixir for which he aspires. Finally, however, he finds
in an old receptacle in his home the clue that will enable him to
interpret the document containing the formula. The box also contains another paper which he does not read, stating ominously that
one of his ancestors had "sold himself to Sathan" and brought upon
the "ancient family" a destiny that had not been "happy or very
prosperous."[62]

That night Septimius is seen pacing to and fro on a distant hill,
waving his hands in diabolic triumph, and "those who listened to his
shrieks said that he was calling to the Devil."[63] By sunrise the next
day Septimius achieves the amalgamation of elements that guaran-
tees the production of the elixir of life. But contemplating the
lonely future that will be his in infinite time, he decides to share
his secret with a girl, Sybil Dacy, who has excited in him a modi-
cum of human affection. In rapture he paints the glorious life
that they will enjoy. His anticipations embrace the flight of centuries, during which he will improve the lot of mankind. Together
they "will contrive deep philosophies, [and] take up one theory
after another. . . ." They "will build a system that shall stand";
they will invent "theories of government" and "fit the people to
govern itself, to do with little government, to do with none."[64] And
finally, after the passage of countless eons of time, Septimius will
become a prophet, "a greater than Mahomet, and will put all man's
hopes into [his] doctrine, and make him good, holy, happy; and he
shall put up his prayers to his Creator, and find them answered,
because they shall be wise. . . ." But then Hawthorne's Faust
chooses a life of wickedness, for he "would experience all." He

imagines himself a murderer, an arch criminal. He, in order to understand truth, "must live these things."[65]

In this magnificent rhapsody of ambition, Septimius surpasses the aspirations of his prototype. Out of the finite into the infinite his mind ventures with supreme confidence. He thinks himself capable of apprehending the total truth of the universe. But, even with his glorious dream of utopian existence, some instinct warns him that he cannot know truth until he experiences evil. Whether Hawthorne intended this inclination to be the catastrophic pitfall that would overcome Septimius on his path to forbidden knowledge, there is no way of knowing, despite the stress on the pedagogic influence of sin in *The Marble Faun*. In any event, chance deals the last card in this game of destiny. Sybil, who is the first to drink the inestimable elixir of life, immediately falls dead. The potion, as she herself knew, was a fatal poison; the sacrifice of her own life was the only way she could teach Septimius the vanity of his experimentation.

Hawthorne purposely leaves Septimius' ultimate fate in doubt. What remorse will visit him after being lifted out of his trance of egoism and error, the imagination may conjecture. In this obscurity lies hidden the core of the greatest novel ever projected by Hawthorne. Perhaps the crucial fault revealed by this draft is the inability to hurdle the hampering obstacle of trying to weld together too many disparate themes. In spite of its shortcomings, the unfinished novel discloses Hawthorne's versatility in handling the formula of the Faust myth. Using the device of the elixir of life, usually termed one of his eccentric Gothic preoccupations, Hawthorne opens up vast fields of speculation, not only on the present destiny of mankind, but on the future course of civilization. That the novel shows the influence of Goethe's *Faust* is no impeachment of Hawthorne's originality. He transforms his borrowings beyond immediate recognition. Septimius Felton is undeniably an American Faust, for his voice, in the perspective of the twentieth century, is prophetic of our own confused pursuit of forbidden knowledge.

CHAPTER X

THE ACHIEVEMENT: A FAUSTIAN PENTACLE

IVE MAJOR ARCS of Faustian definition merge to describe the full circle of Hawthorne's prodigious achievement in literature. As if a portent of the precise character of his mythic technique, the five points of juncture establish the inner form of his art, for they mark the design of a pentacle: the magical symbol of Faustian conjuration. The arcs, in another turn of the metaphor, represent the five distinct rhythms of Hawthorne's creative imagination: the modulations of a harmonious composition of myth that envelop the total destiny of historical and natural man. For, in essence, the devil-archetype recaptures the lost significance of evil in the equation of human life. As did mythopoeic man, Hawthorne manipulates the educative image to achieve a reconciliation of the destructive dualism of good and evil that has shattered the moral vision of Western civilization. Probing remorselessly into the psychological motivations underlying typical responses to experience with evil, he translates the implications of these reactions into immutable ethical values which link man to man and forge the magnetic chain of humanity. To the degree that the individual recognizes the clash of good and evil as the tragic condition of his existence, Hawthorne contends, he acquires the self-knowledge that releases the flow of vital love into the endless stream of life. In sum, by willingly accepting the responsibilities of *all* choices of conduct, he sacrifices his personal ego to the greater demands of his active role in society as a contributor to its stabilizing energies. Thus, in a unique symbolic idiom Hawthorne expounds a philosophy for living that parallels the message of Christ's parables.

This conception of the enveloping purpose of Hawthorne's art permits an evaluation of his total production in terms of a gradually expanding vision of man's spiritual plight. Tales, sketches, legends, allegories, moralities, mysteries, and romances: each category forms a tier in a vast symbolic structure, and each is susceptible of a meaningful interpretation within the framework of his ethical formula. The specific narrative mode denotes no more than a particular approach of the moment to the omnipresent problem of good and evil. This investigation is launched even in the tentative and experimental line of action in *Fanshawe,* the initial extension of Hawthorne's primary creative arc. Critics have long been confounded by the optimism or arrogance which impelled him to publish at his own expense this so-called artistic mediocrity. Dismissed contemptuously as an imitation of the sentimental novel, the work has never received proper consideration in the perspective which shaped its intention. The youthful author, a dissenter from the novelistic tradition of his times — the prevailing sentimental and the emergent realistic — actually experiments with a symbolic technique in *Fanshawe.* That he had the narrative ability to do so is attested by such short stories as "The Hollow of the Three Hills" and "Young Goodman Brown," which follow closely upon the novel.

Either of two factors perhaps explains the negative reaction of contemporary readers and critics to the work: an apparently abortive execution of thematic purpose, or an inert imaginative response to an unfamiliar fictional technique. *Fanshawe* does not embody the conventions of the sentimental novel of that day; hence it can be criticized on the basis of received standards. On the other hand, if a symbolic experiment, the effort defies the current literary tradition which provides the reader with his interpretative tools. Therefore Hawthorne's public is again absolved of artistic ignorance. The modern critic, however, stands indicted. Hawthorne provides him with all the clues to a rewarding appraisal of theme on both the literal and symbolic levels of the plot.

In the first instance, the ironic epigraphs to each of the ten chapters explicitly enunciate the serio-comic nature of the theme in the body of the story. Quotations, for example, from Shakespeare and Scott, when examined in the context of the original sources, advocate attitudes toward love directly opposed to Fanshawe's. In effect, Hawthorne, on the literal or historical level of the plot, denounces the dangers of sentimentalizing basic human emotions. As this theme broadens in the symbolic penumbra of the work, it reveals his concern with emotional stagnation. Though he uses a subdued Faustian investiture — associations with *Melmoth the Wanderer* — to intensify the conflict between good and evil, the controlling mythic ideology of the devil emerges by analogy in color symbolism — black, gray, and white, which he affiliates respectively with Butler, Ellen, and Fanshawe. Ellen's normal emotional predispositions contrast sharply with the two extremes: Butler's primitive selfishness and Fanshawe's sterile virtue. Only in the middle way, Ellen's integration of all the implications of experience, does Hawthorne perceive the reconciliation of good and evil — of love channeled into the fruitfulness of life.

Misread as *Fanshawe* was and still is, it is no wonder, then, that Hawthorne withdraws the work from the public market. Swallowing his humiliation and frustration, however, he almost immediately centers upon the historical setting for his stories that will allow him to exercise his symbolic talents. Puritan history provides him with a fictional theatre that is remote enough in time to sanction imaginative freedom with fact, yet familiar enough to convey the illusion of truth. Moreover, the culture bequeaths him the mythic image which interprets its members' status amid the forces of good and evil in the world: the devil-archetype. Hawthorne therefore proceeds to extend still further the creative arc inaugurated with *Fanshawe*. The color symbolism of black and white ceases to be a mere personification of evil. Enforced by the concrete emblem of the Puritan's view of the destructive principle in the moral universe, the original symbolic formulation attains a dramatic, compelling tone. But unlike his progenitors Hawthorne strives to explain the significance of the devil-image in psychological, not theological, terms. He probes behind the concealing veils of dogma, and discovers in this verbal darkness the cowering soul of the founding fathers of New England. As they disguised their fear of evil in militant bigotry and rigorous outward piety, so they secretly paid homage to the devil who gleefully lashed their disoriented consciences. This awareness of the grievous rift in the moral citadel of Puritan civilization incites Hawthorne to write its spiritual history in the semblance of his fictional tales.

While respecting the historical reality to the extent of only a vague "authenticity of . . . outline,"[1] he recaptures in his invented circumstances more of the natural history of the times than do all the voluminous chroniclers of the period. History lives in his characters. The impersonal incident of a Quaker persecution or a Black Mass, he realizes, is embalmed history, for only in the reactions of specific individuals who live the transient events do we see the reflection of past experience. Their thoughts and their emotions constitute the history of an occurrence, not the occurrence itself. As the diary of Samuel Sewall fascinates us by its unself-conscious revelations of deviation from Puritan disciplines, so Hawthorne's candid interpolations of the patterns of Puritan behavior engage our attention. The blush that a confession by Sewall brings to the cheek springs from the same common human nature that the Salem artist focuses on. But even more acutely than we perceive the devilish temptations which gnawed hungrily at Sewall's moral convictions, we experience Hawthorne's sensitive re-creation of the decline and disintegration of Puritan civilization. We cannot help it. Unknowingly, his prophetic insight embraces the modern world, its tragic moral dislocations and its loss of hope.

In four tales he isolates the seeds of dissolution that will germinate into a blighting weed in the garden of Puritan moral idealism. Recognizing the pure motives which moved these immigrants to exile themselves from their native land, he laments the disunity that threatens from "the deformity of any government that does not grow out of the nature of things. . . ."[2] This sentiment pervades "The Gray Champion." The symbolic patriarch of the community, the gray champion, arises out of the valley of death in an hour of impending catastrophe to warn against the populace's belief that "Satan will strike his master-stroke presently. . . ."[3] He succeeds in welding the people together in a solidarity of spirit that frightens off the enemy, but, as Hawthorne casually remarks at the end of the story, each succeeding generation of "New England's sons [must] vindicate their ancestry."[4] Unfortunately the growth of religious bigotry, he points out again, renders this hope improbable. For in "The Gentle Boy" he observes the tendency of his forebears to project the demon of intolerance within their own breasts upon scapegoats in the outer world. So diseased is this attitude that it rejects normal human sympathy and compassion; emotions freeze, as he indicates, into the *snowy* sterility of coldness and indifference: the devil's tragic deficiency of feeling. This communal predisposition will, of course, infect individuals, and Hawthorne traces the consequences in "Young Goodman Brown." Overcome by his own self-righteousness, the hero of this parable renounces wife, children, and community to brood upon his own sanctimonious piety. He dotes upon the devil of hypocrisy that coddles his conscience. Finally New England's exquisite historian of Puritan moral sensibilities daringly exposes the sexual phobias of his ancestors in the phallic symbolism of "The Maypole of Merry Mount." He uncovers in this investigation the abnormal character of their moral disciplines: their incompatibility with ordinary human nature. Again they are victims of the deceitful devil of their dogmatic theology who shames them into fear and humiliation, casting the aura of evil over the normal expression of deep emotion, even within the bonds of holy wedlock.

Numerous other tales written in this first period of creative originality broaden Hawthorne's canvas of the Puritan soul in conflict with the devil. But nowhere, except in fleeting intuitions, does any individual challenge the role of the demon in the moral life of the community; rather there is a collective surrender to the mythic symbol of evil. The retreat into sanctimonious spiritual pride and belligerently aggressive piety marks the rationalization of a vulnerable moral cowardice. The interaction with the devil, which should breed self-awareness and humility, instead inspires complacency and arrogance. The Puritan soul fails to realize that its exaltation of the devil-archetype verges on blasphemy. The conquest of religious light — love, charity, tolerance, and humility — by the dark clouds of pessimism and gloom presage the death of the culture. In the implications of this aspect of the Faust cycle Hawthorne anticipates Arnold J. Toynbee's speculations on the formula of history. Like the historian, the writer affirms that the struggle between good and evil or between God and Satan can be resolved only through an understanding of evil: a recognition that the challenge of evil must animate and invigorate the latent good in the throbbing heart of mankind.[5]

Having unfolded the spiritual history of his own ancestors in settings largely imaginary yet suggestively realistic, Hawthorne now ventures on occasion into completely symbolic backgrounds. The quest of the ambitious guest or of Peter Goldthwaite or of the obsessed pilgrims in "The Great Carbuncle" are ritual lines of action, for, whoever the hero, he searches the world or his heart for the clue that will reveal his role in life. If, however, he deludes himself with the devil's promises that the good is an external value, he succumbs to a self-deception that precludes insight into self. He accomplishes his own doom.

In this first development of the circle of his Faust myth Hawthorne denies salvation to his major protagonists, as he does to the culture which sold its soul to the devil. Where no inward candle of truth flickers even waveringly to illuminate the sinister inclinations of the heart, there can reside neither the nobility nor the dignity that confers upon man's helpless struggle against himself and circumstance the mantle of tragic destiny. His fate parallels Lucifer's: devouring aspirations gorge themselves upon his emotions, leaving within the soul the empty coldness of freely chosen exile from the human family. Without ethical values, he is a philosopher without a philosophy. He is irredeemably lost.

The creative arc next traced by Hawthorne envelops deeper dimensions of universal reality. For the most part, the backgrounds of his stories are as vague and unreal as those of all racial mythologies — from the earliest recorded myths of man to those articulated today by the American Indians. Milieu dissipates into nothing, for action predominates along with character, both of which are unimpeachably symbolic. Though still concerned with the psychological motivations which shape human behavior, the confident artist now creates a hierarchy of heroes, each of whose attitudes and aspirations in their materialization into action illuminates a contemporary way of life. At the same time these distinctive configurations of human action refract the guiding values which are disorienting the development of nineteenth-century American civilization. These characters comprise Hawthorne's gallery of five Fausts.

Coincidentally, as in Goethe's *Faust,* a woman stands at the crossroads of destiny in each crucial endeavor of these five Fausts, pointing the way toward the self-knowledge that will return them to the precincts of common humanity and will perhaps reconcile the contradictory impulses within their hearts. Georgiana in "The Birthmark" and Beatrice in "Rappaccini's Daughter" are counterparts of the mythic spiritual guides who attempt to lead those heroes chosen for great destinies toward the goals most beneficial to society. Aylmer, for instance, personifies all the aspirations of nineteenth-century science, in particular the illusion of perfectionism to which it gave birth. On the threshold of its first fruitful development, its protagonist, Aylmer, charts a course that will lead to inevitable doom, a fate which the atomic and hydrogen bombs seem to confirm. Rejecting the implicit advice of Georgiana that he reconcile his experiments to ends consistent with humanity, he sacrifices her to his megalomaniacal pretensions. Symbolically this ruthless act discloses the impersonal and inhuman objectivity of science, for, as Hawthorne describes Aylmer's conduct at Georgiana's deathbed, the latter is more interested in her pulse beat than in saving her life. Though she voluntarily chooses death in order to guide Aylmer to truth, she fails in her mission, as Christ has apparently failed. Thus Hawthorne warns that scientific perfectionism will destroy itself as long as it persists in separating its ultimate aims from human love.

Similarly, Beatrice in Rappaccini's new Eden symbolizes the selfless love that must inspire the scientist in his quest toward truth. In this garden of inverted values she preserves an inner humility and nobility that neither Rappaccini nor Giovanni in their egocentricity can recognize. Poisoned less by her father's flowers than by the envenomed love of parent and suitor, she also elects death to point out the necessity of human love in all pursuits. And again Hawthorne denounces another aspect of cold-hearted Faustian science in his day.

The two Fausts of "The Artist of the Beautiful" and "Drowne's Wooden Image" illustrate the predicament of the creative mind in a materialistic and utilitarian society: whether to worship the inner ideal or compromise with outer conventions. In the first instance Owen Warland perceives that the soul-image transcends any current standard of infatuation — such as is exemplified by Annie Hovendon, who serves as an ephemeral substitute. Conversely, Drowne, who is granted the legacy of a Pygmalion, never apprehends that his failure to retain an inspiration lies with his inability to substitute an inner ideal for the momentary vision of an outer. Whereas Drowne relapses into the mediocrity of conventional tastes, Warland, much like Hawthorne, remains faithful to his inspiration, defying the workaday world to darken the light within. Warland's artistic integrity parallels that of his creator, for both were forced to conquer the Mephistophelian derogations of their critics. For it is the tendency of blunted sensibilities to deny excellence to anything difficult to understand, and where the criteria of value are monetary and utilitarian the frustrations of the artist are multiplied. Such were the conditions during most of Hawthorne's writing career.

The magnificent stature of the fifth Faust defines the intention of Hawthorne's myth: to elaborate a philosophy of life that reconciles the highest intellectual endeavors with the value-feelings exalted by the masses of mankind. The shadowy feminine character who initiates Ethan Brand's journey around the world stands, like the Margaret of Goethe's *Faust,* as the symbol of the cohesive principle in the world. When at last he returns to his lime-kiln in the throes of an expiatory despair, he virtually asserts the claim of his Margaret.

He declares that one cannot trample upon the universal heart of mankind, the reservoir of unquenchable love that feeds the mighty stream of life. This realization of his guilt, the unpardonable sin, encompasses so crucial a truth that Ethan Brand considers its apprehension, despite its consequences, the most significant attainment of his life. In this pronouncement Hawthorne pessimistically prophesies the decay of his own culture whose vision of sustaining values approximates the civilization of the Puritans in its period of decline. All history, he thus implies, teaches a similar lesson: the ethics of universal love alone must determine the concrete external values of the community or the state.

In this second phase of creative development Hawthorne's other works, regardless of their narrative form, provide a background of commentary on the five Fausts. A frail sketch like "Mrs. Bullfrog," for instance, is a farcical treatment of the theme of perfectionism which animates "The Birthmark." In a similar fashion "Egotism; or, the Bosom Serpent" is a particular illustration of the emotional stagnation that colors the scientific aspirations of the Rappaccinis of the world. Significantly, the majority of the short pieces rely upon some extension of the devil-archetype to resolve their plots, and cumulatively comment upon the gallery of Fausts.

Hawthorne's virtuosity at this point looks forward to a crystallization of his symbolic technique in another narrative field. His control of the Faust myth in the short fiction clearly indicates this new creative direction, and the experiment with "Ethan Brand" offers concrete proof of his toying with a new inspiration. Inevitably he dreams of the masterpiece that has haunted the literary imagination of American writers, from Washington Irving to Henry Wadsworth Longfellow, the delineation of an American Faust who will express the aspirations of the young republic. But apparently dissatisfied with the all-inclusive dimensions of such a figure, he returns to the fountainhead of his earliest Faustian stories — the Puritan scene. And against this background he darkly paints the tragic figure of a New England Faust. So Hawthorne's genius, now in its mature third phase, attains a climactic fulfillment.

But the historical setting of *The Scarlet Letter* does not stereotype Hawthorne's Faust, nor does it localize the implications of the action to Puritan times. For, in truth, the outward movement of the plot borrows its glow from the light shed on the inward life of the characters — not, however, as they simulate Puritan introspection, but as they reflect the traits of common human nature. Hester is not merely a reluctantly penitent adulteress; she epitomizes womanhood. She enacts the universal role of a woman deeply and passionately in love, by instinctive cunning seeking security for herself and her illegitimate child through the man to whom she has given her heart. Nor is Chillingworth merely a satanic puppet; he is everyman. He dehumanizes his emotions upon the tyrannical commands of his wounded ego. Similiarly, Dimmesdale wears the cloth of his profession, but his predicament is characteristically human, as the spirit and the flesh contend for victory. And Pearl, who desperately seeks the status of filial identity as instinctively as Hester her station, is a demonic child only for readers who have been improperly weaned from fairy tales. Therefore the natural history of human emotions which Hawthorne dramatizes through the inner lives of his characters reduces the historical setting to the insignificance of the makeshift props in a Shakespearean theatre.

Hawthorne's Faust, Chillingworth, rationalizes his obsessive vengefulness into religious predestination, while in reality this conclusion merely demonstrates the limitations of rigid intellectuality. Like the typical Faust, he substitutes abstract principles of conduct for value-feelings which only the heart can determine, especially when the issue is love. To this degree only is he a villain and the counterpart of his creator's other misguided aspirants for pure truth: Rappaccini, Aylmer, and Ethan Brand. But when finally deprived of human emotions, he is indeed a devil, the embodiment of cold, functionless thought and the disciple of the Black Man of Puritan mythology. For this is the demon who educates his antagonists to hate those very qualities which, lacking, estrange him from heaven — humility, love, pity, and compassion. Thus Chillingworth, whose Faustian talents appear to promise emancipation from provincial hypocrisy, ironically cannot escape the emotional frigidity of his devouter brethren. His mind overrules his heart, dogma theirs. Therein lies the tragic fate of the Puritan Faust.

Chillingworth's inability to reconcile the arrogant demands of his intellect to the charitable impulses of his heart contrasts with the experience of Hester and Dimmesdale. On the one hand, her instinctive desires, as tyrannically insistent as her husband's cold thoughts, isolate her more and more from society. She refuses to compromise with her animal nature, resisting contact with the devil in her thoughts. Only on her final submissive return to the community does she acknowledge and accept her guilt with all its consequences, conquering the evil within herself with a gift of sincere and benevolent love that flows into the stream of community life. Though less heroic than Hester, Dimmesdale also defeats the tormenting devil of the flesh who beguiles him into spiritual hypocrisy, for in his rejection of Hester he reaffirms his loyalty to the moral code of his profession. And his confession of parenthood readmits both himself and his daughter into the human family. Conforming to Hawthorne's principle of the educative function of evil, Hester and Dimmesdale acquire along with self-knowledge a humble selflessness. They realize that love must adapt its demands to the inner and outer realities of existence, not only completing the individual personality, but also insuring the individual's status in the human community.

Despite the fact that the characters resolve their fates within a Puritan environment, they resolve them as typical human beings, not Puritans. The moral values ultimately espoused by Hester and Dimmesdale are not the exclusive possession of any religious sect. They belong to humanity. They proclaim the sanctity of universal love on the authority of human nature — the truth which Hawthorne's Faust overlooks. Thus the greatness of *The Scarlet Letter* derives from the author's insights into plights of the spirit that are common to the experience of mankind. The moral dilemma of a Hester or a Dimmesdale is not restricted in time or place. It is the fate of any man or woman who defies the taboos of a society, while at the same time violating the sacred role of a mother or a priest.

The sweep of Hawthorne's third creative arc, sustained in its sensitive investigation of inner life by the archetypal devil-image and the ritual of selling the soul, begins to close the Faust circle, and his fourth stage of achievement betrays a less intensive note of tragic earnestness. *The House of the Seven Gables* and *The Blithedale Romance* reflect this relaxation. He does not, however, dispense with the symbolic machinery of the Faust myth, for the pre-narrative motivation of a devil's curse implements the immediate action. The intention of the former novel, never swerving "aside from the truth of the human heart,"[6] reveals Hawthorne's continuing concern with the necessity of reconciling extremes. Phoebe, the embodiment of natural spontaneity and good will, mediates the ancestral pretensions of the aristocratic Pyncheons and the arrogant pride of the humble Maules, neutralizing generations of hostility. In the process the icy evil of clannishness melts into the common stream of love that invigorates the life of the community. At the same time, again going beyond the literal level of the plot, Hawthorne denounces the stratification of society according to birth and wealth, and proscribes these aristocratic anachronisms as the danger threatening the vitality of democracy and of Christian brotherhood — inequalities especially flagrant in the New England of his day.

With a perspective still on contemporary society, *The Blithedale Romance* castigates sentimental utopianism, short cuts to knowledge (mesmerism), and zealous social reform. But these attacks on the current foibles of man subsume Hawthorne's basic preoccupation with common human nature, especially with the satanic negations of self-interest. The uncompromising idealism of Hollingsworth, the Mephistophelian opportunism of Westervelt, and even the protective reserve of Coverdale symptomized the spiritual maladies of the diseased optimism of the age. Proclaiming evil an illusion, the custodians of a revered Puritan heritage defiantly laugh away the moral gloom of their ancestors. They deny the existence of the devil. But, as Hawthorne grimly intimates, this is wishful thinking. Behind this extreme belief in providential benevolence are secreted the pitfalls of Satan. Inverting the spiritual outlook of the Puritans, this New England generation repeats the error of the past: it ignores the immutable texture of human nature, defining its values in terms of false ideals. Mankind, Hawthorne implies, can neither deify the devil nor minimize his power. The evil principle must be recognized for what it is: the mythic creation of the psyche of western civilization — the warning from a collective instinct that evil must be met and conquered.

This lack of awareness of the nature of evil permeates the substance of the two novels. It reveals an incapacity of the contemporary soul to recognize the tragic sense of experience. Hawthorne portrays his fellow men as they are and as the times dictate. He denies their optimism the richness of a full life. Reality eludes them because they do not reckon with its primary colors of black and white.

Hawthorne never permits his world to forget this truth. Years later, as the fifth arc of his Faust myth closes the circle of a unified symbolic structure of fiction, he resoundingly declares that evil alone can teach man a vital morality. *The Marble Faun* merely reiterates what Hawthorne perhaps failed to articulate clearly in *Fanshawe* — and, tragically, what he attempted to exalt in the unfinished romances as a universal Faust myth. The last complete novel relegates the ideal of a Golden Age to the limbo of a saint's innocent dream. Donatello, whose innocuous rapport with nature is eclipsed by evil, actually begins to realize his human destiny only after he sins. Then, paradoxically, he becomes part of the world of process which is nature. In his soul he recapitulates the inexorable cycle of birth, death, and rebirth: the vision of reality that Hawthorne dared to elaborate in his fiction. And at the same time the spiritual growth of Donatello distinctly parallels the myths which relate the trials and tribulations of the great prophets of religious illumination — from Buddha to Christ. But the enlightenment comes to Donatello through Miriam, for she teaches him the wisdom of selflessness, the knowledge that awakens the dead soul at the threshold of rebirth. Ironically, Hilda, like her Puritan forebears, lingers the longest before the challenge that confronts the others — that the devil conquered, the fear of fear mastered, constitutes the only healthy state of the spirit. Enacted against the symbolic background of the labyrinths which sheltered the first Christian converts, the drama of *The Marble Faun* therefore climactically punctuates Hawthorne's deep devotion to the ethics of Jesus Christ — his profound belief that a self-denying love is the linking force in human solidarity.

To move from this latter work into the innumerable drafts and scenarios of the projected Faust myth is to voyage through the chaotic seas of an imagination caught in the storms of a mighty inspiration. Though the magnificent intention of the creative impulse does not materialize into a finished work, the fragments, long and short, haunt the sensitive mind like the memory of the scattered remains of a noble Gothic cathedral. Indeed the mixture of the grotesque and dignified in the titles of the manuscripts, *Doctor Grimshawe's Secret, The Dolliver Romance,* and *Septimius Felton,* recalls the incongruities of the medieval churches. As unseemly gargoyles and contorted buttresses without magnify the graceful architectural perspectives within, so the magic elixirs, demonic spiders, poisonous flowers, and bloody footprints, the external symbols of Hawthorne's Faust myth, call attention to the subtler beauty of implied thought. For associations from Goethe's *Faust* merge with Hawthorne's own conceptions of a heroic age of the future to open new vistas of speculation that enchant and terrify the imagination. This holds true especially for *Septimius Felton.* The implications of this work anticipate the wild Faustian convulsions of the twentieth century — from the designs of world conquest by Hitler and Stalin to the Fausts of the atomic laboratories who have almost attained to the knowledge of the creative principle in the universe. But underneath these fabulous notions, the solemn and profound intellect of Hawthorne contemplates the moral life of man. The conflict of good and evil never fades from his vision of the future. Nor does human nature change, nor the condition of mankind's salvation. But on the brink of catastrophe the selfless spirit always waits, ready to sacrifice itself: in its willing death insuring life.

On this tragic conviction the resplendent cycle of Hawthorne's genius closes. Short stories and novels all unite effectively to elaborate the formula of human destiny in the interaction of God and the devil. Man must meet the challenge of the devil by recognizing his existence. He must accept the myth of the devil as one of the hidden structures of psychic reality. Only then will he apprehend truth.

NOTES

CHAPTER I

1. Nathaniel Hawthorne in *The Complete Works of Nathaniel Hawthorne,* with introductory notes by George Parsons Lathrop, 13 vols. (Riverside Edition; Boston: Houghton, Mifflin and Co., 1883), III, 442. Hereafter this edition will be cited merely as *Complete Works.*
2. *Ibid.,* III, 447–448.
3. *Ibid.,* I, 16.
4. *Ibid.,* V, 54–55.
5. Among the works which elaborate this aspect of Hawthorne's art are "A Select Party" (*ibid.,* II, 70–88), "Monsieur du Miroir" (*ibid.,* II, 182–195), "The Hall of Fantasy" (*ibid.,* II, 196–211), and also the preface to "Rappaccini's Daughter" (*ibid.,* II, 107–109).
6. *Ibid.,* XII, 109.
7. *Ibid.,* II, 107–108.
8. *Ibid.,* III, 386.
9. *Ibid.,* III, 386.
10. Carl G. Jung, *Contributions to Analytical Psychology,* trans. H. G. and Cary F. Baynes (New York: Harcourt, Brace and Company, 1928), p. 247. (Quoted by permission of the Bollingen Foundation, the present copyright owner.)
11. T. S. Eliot, *The Cocktail Party* (New York: Harcourt, Brace and Company, 1950), p. 184.
12. Arnold J. Toynbee, *A Study of History* (London: Oxford University Press, 1939), I, 271. Toynbee's reduction of t growth and decline of civilizations to a formula of challenge and response closely parallels Hawthorne's conception of the function of evil in human existence; moreover, along with the latter, the historian accepts the mythic archetype of the devil as an indispensable educative symbol (*ibid.,* I, 271–299). As the characters in Hawthorne's fiction confront the challenge of evil with varying degrees of self-awareness, so, according to Toynbee, do the individuals in a specific society: "As ordeal follows ordeal, some members of society at some moment fail altogether to adjust themselves, and fall by the way; others struggle on, strained or warped or stunted; others grow in wisdom and stature, and in making their own way discover new avenues for a general advance of the society to which they belong" (*ibid.,* I, 23).

CHAPTER II

1. *Complete Works,* V, 25.
2. Included among them were such classics as *De Praestigiis Daemonum* by Joannes Wierus, *Operae Horae Subsecivae* by Joachim Camerarius, *Selectae Disputationes Theologicae* by

Voetius, and *The Wonders of the Little World* by Nathaniel Wanley. See J. A. Walz, "Increase Mather and Dr. Faust, an American 'Faustsplitter,'" *Germanic Review,* XV (1940), 29–30.

3. See E. M. Butler's *The Myth of the Magus* (New York: The Macmillan Company, 1948).

4. Thomas G. Wright, *Literary Culture in New England* (New Haven: Yale University Press, 1920), pp. 121–123.

5. Increase Mather, *Cases of Conscience* (London: Reeves and Turner, 1890), p. 271.

6. Quoted by Ralph Barton Perry, in *Puritanism and Democracy* (New York: The Vanguard Press, 1944), p. 233.

7. William Rose, ed. *The Famous History of Dr. Faustus, 1592–1594* (New York: E. P. Dutton & Company, n.d.), p. 180.

8. *Ibid.,* p. 76.

9. Perry, p. 85.

10. J. H. Tuttle, "The Libraries of the Mathers," *Proceedings of The American Antiquarian Society,* N.S. 1, XX (1909–1910), 269–356.

11. Quoted in George L. Burr, ed. *Narratives of the Witchcraft Cases* (New York: Barnes & Noble, Inc., 1914), pp 137–138. The quotation is from *Memorable Providences, Relating to Witchcraft Possessions* (1689).

12. *Complete Works,* IV, 512–514.

CHAPTER III

1. Scott H. Goodnight, *German Literature in American Magazines Prior to 1846,* University of Wisconsin Bulletin No. 203, 1908. The author lists an impressive number of translations that appeared in periodicals all over the country to substantiate the attribution of considerable popularity and influence to German literary thought in America.

2. Albert E. Baugh, ed. *A Literary History of England* (New York: Appleton-Century-Crofts, Inc., 1946), p. 1406. Longfellow, for instance, knew both translations. See O. W. Long, "Goethe and Longfellow," *Germanic Review,* VII (1932), 166.

3. Thomas Roscoe, *The German Novelists,* 4 vols. (London, 1826).

4. Henry A. Pochmann, "Irving's German Tour and Its Influence on His Tales," *Publications of the Modern Language Association,* XLV (1930), 1186.

5. *Complete Works,* V, 43.

6. *Cambridge History of American Literature* (New York: The Macmillan Company, 1946), I, 343.

7. Mason Wade, ed. *The Writings of Margaret Fuller* (New York: The Viking Press, 1941), pp. 252–254.

8. Randall Stewart, ed. *The American Notebooks by Nathaniel Hawthorne* (New Haven: Yale University Press, 1932), p. 157. Hereafter this work will be cited merely as *American Notebooks.*

9. *Complete Works,* IV, 135–136.

10. *Ibid.,* IV, 13.

11. Marion L. Kesselring, *Hawthorne's Reading, 1828–1850* (New York: The New York Public Library, 1949), p. 84.

12. Pochmann, 1186.
13. Washington Irving, *The Works of Washington Irving* (New York: G. P. Putnam & Company, 1854–56), VII, 393–419.
14. G. S. Hellman, *Washington Irving* (New York: Alfred A. Knopf, 1925) pp. 165–167.
15. J. T. Hatfield, *New Light on Longfellow with Special Reference to His Relations in Germany* (Boston: Houghton Mifflin Company, 1933), p. 56.
16. O. W. Long, "Goethe and Longfellow," *Germanic Review,* VII (1932), pp. 166–167.
17. *Ibid.,* 167.
18. See Samuel Longfellow, *Henry Wadsworth Longfellow* (Boston: Houghton, Mifflin and Company, 1883), I, 276.
19. *Ibid.,* I, 260.
20. *Ibid.,* I, 290–291.
21. *Ibid.,* I, 292–293.
22. *Ibid.,* I, 311.
23. *Ibid.,* I, 279–318, *passim.*
24. *Ibid.,* I, p. 299*n.*
25. Frank P. Stearns, *The Life and Genius of Nathaniel Hawthorne* (Boston: Richard C. Badger, 1906), p. 133.
26. Longfellow, I, 354.
27. Herbert W. Schneider, *The Puritan Mind* (New York: Henry Holt and Company, 1930), p. 262.
28. *Complete Works,* I, 220.
29. *Ibid.,* I, 16.
30. Herman Melville, "Hawthorne and His Mosses," in Edmund Wilson's collection *The Shock of Recognition* (New York: Doubleday, Doran & Company, 1943), pp. 187–204.
31. Louise Tharp, *The Peabody Sisters of Salem* (Boston: Little, Brown and Company, 1950), pp. 133–135.

32. Barret Wendell, *A Literary History of America* (New York: Charles Scribner's Sons, 1911), p. 296.
33. C. S. Coad, "The Gothic Element in American Literature Before 1835," *Journal of English and Germanic Philology,* XXIV (1925), 72–76.

CHAPTER IV

1. William Rose, *The Famous History of Dr. Faustus,* p. 47.
2. William Beckford in *Vathek* (New York: The F. M. Lupton Publishing Company, n.d.), pp. 176–192.
3. The ramifications of this motif are explored in Eino Railo's *The Haunted Castle: A Study of the Elements of English Romanticism* (New York: E. P. Dutton & Company, 1937) and in Mario Praz's *The Romantic Agony* (London: Oxford University Press, 1933).
4. William Godwin, *Caleb Williams, or Things as They Are* (London: George Routledge & Sons, 1903), p. 27. Charles Brockden Brown's *Arthur Mervyn,* one of America's first Gothic novels, develops the psychological perversions of extreme curiosity in a manner similar to Godwin. See Harry R. Warfel's *Charles Brockden Brown* (Gainesville: University of Florida Press, 1949), pp. 143–144.
5. Montague Summers, *The Gothic Quest* (London: The Fortune Press, 1938), p. 26.
6. Newton Arvin, ed. *The Heart of Hawthorne's Journals* (Bos-

ton: Houghton Mifflin Company, 1929), p. 7.

7. Charles Robert Maturin, *Melmoth the Wanderer* (London: Charles Bentley, 1892), III, 257.

8. *Ibid.*, III, 261.

9. See George William MacArthur Reynolds, *Faust* (London: George Vickers, 1847), p. 4. The novel was first serialized in the *London Journal* from October, 1845, to July, 1846.

10. E. T. A. Hoffmann, *The Devil's Elixir* (London: T. Caldwell, 1824), I, 153. The novel was first published in Germany in 1816 as *Die Elixire des Teufels*. The first English translation appeared in *Blackwood's Edinburgh Magazine* in 1824. The same year it also came out in book form. See Bayard Q. Morgan's *A Critical Bibliography of German Literature in English Translation, 1461–1927* (Palo Alto: Stanford University Press, 1938), p. 162.

11. *Complete Works,* V, 234.

12. Hoffmann, I, 157.

13. *Ibid.*, I, 155.

14. *Ibid.*, I, 157.

15. *Complete Works,* V, 205.

16. Hoffmann, I, 161.

17. *Ibid.*, II, 5.

18. *Complete Works,* III, 532.

19. Honoré de Balzac, *Philosophical Studies,* in *The Novels of Honoré de Balzac,* trans. G. Burnham Ives (Philadelphia: George Barrie & Son, 1899), II, 45.

20. *Ibid.*, II, 82–83.

21. *Ibid.*, V, 109.

22. *Ibid.*, I, 240.

23. *Ibid.*, I, 340.

24. *Ibid.*, I, 363.

25. *Complete Works,* II, 379.

26. Quoted in Randall Stewart, *Nathaniel Hawthorne: A Biography* (New Haven: Yale University Press, 1948), pp. 27–28.

27. *Ibid.,* p. 8.

28. George Parsons Lathrop, *A Study of Hawthorne* (Boston: Houghton, Mifflin and Company, 1876), p. 146.

29. Kesselring, *Hawthorne's Reading,* p. 45.

30. Summers, *The Gothic Quest,* p. 367.

CHAPTER V

1. *Complete Works,* III, 13.

2. *Ibid.*, XI, 108.

3. *Ibid.*, XI, 92.

4. See Christopher Marlowe's *The Tragical History of Doctor Faustus,* Act I, Scene I, 97, reprinted in *Eight Elizabethan Plays* (New York: The Modern Library, 1932).

5. *Complete Works,* XI, 88.

6. *Ibid.*, XI, 93.

7. Gower's translation of *Faust* was first published in 1823, but there is no proof available that it had any general circulation at this time in the literary circles of New England.

8. *Complete Works,* XI, 93.

9. *Ibid.*, XI, 215.

10. *Ibid.*, XI, 217.

11. E. L. Chandler, "Hawthorne's 'Spectator,'" in *New England Quarterly,* IV (1931), 293.

12. Hawthorne's sister Elizabeth first saw the manuscript of "Alice Doane's Appeal" in the summer of 1825. Even at that time it had been rejected by several publishers (Julian Hawthorne, *Nathaniel Hawthorne and his Wife* [Boston: Houghton, Mifflin and Company,

1884], I, 125). Since the plot of "The Hollow of the Three Hills" is clearly related to the first tale, the two stories are probably the surviving members of the "Seven Tales of My Native Land," whose history Lathrop briefly outlines in the introductory note to *Twice-Told Tales* (*Complete Works*, I, 7). In the introduction to the study of "Alice Doane's Appeal," Hawthorne lists it as one of the two tales that escaped the "brighter destiny . . . of flames" (*ibid.*, XII, 282).

13. *Ibid.*, XII, 287–288.
14. *Ibid.*, I, 229.
15. This setting, in the grammar of the mythic image, might be called an archetypal location.
16. *Complete Works*, III, 575.
17. C. Day Lewis, *The Poetic Image* (London: Jonathan Cape, 1947), p. 32.
18. *Complete Works*, XII, 29.
19. *Ibid.*, XII, 40.
20. *Ibid.*, XII, 41.
21. Hawthorne, review of J. G. Whittier, *The Supernaturalism of New England,* in the *Literary World,* I (April 17, 1847), 247–248. Quoted here by permission of Mr. Manning Hawthorne from the original manuscript in the Berg Collection of the New York Public Library.
22. E. L. Chandler's *A Study of the Sources of the Tales and Romances Written by Nathaniel Hawthorne before 1853,* Smith College Studies in Modern Languages, VII, No. 4 (Northampton, Mass.: 1926) offers a chronology of most of Hawthorne's early works, including all those mentioned in this chapter. These dates are ac-

cepted, in most instances, in this study.
23. *Complete Works*, I, 70.
24. *Ibid.*, I, 78.
25. *Ibid.*, I. 80.
26. *Ibid.*, I, 81.
27. *Ibid.*, I, 82.
28. *Ibid.*, II, 89.
29. *Ibid.*, II, 99.
30. *Ibid.*, II, 104.
31. Hawthorne conveniently stigmatizes his Cain-branded actors in this way.
32. *Complete Works*, I, 100.
33. *Ibid.*, I, 101.
34. *Ibid.*, I, 112.
35. *Ibid.*, I, 119.

CHAPTER VI

1. The tales and sketches considered in this chapter were written between 1830 and 1842; most of them were included in the two editions of *Twice-Told Tales* (1837, 1842).
2. *Complete Works*, I, 346.
3. *Ibid.*, I, 347.
4. *Ibid.*, I, 348.
5. *Ibid.*, II, 194.
6. *Ibid.*, II, 195.
7. *Ibid.*, I, 405.
8. *Ibid.*, I, 433.
9. *Ibid.*, I, 440.
10. *Ibid.*, I, 442.
11. *Ibid.*, II, 153.
12. *Ibid.*, I, 368.
13. *Ibid.*, I, 369.
14. *Ibid.*, I, 367.
15. *Ibid.*, I, 528.
16. *Ibid.*, I, 527.
17. Edward McCurdy, *Leonardo da Vinci's Notebooks* (New York: Empire State Book Company, 1923), p. 8.
18. *Complete Works*, I, 192.
19. *Ibid.*, I, 195.

20. *Ibid.*, I, 206.
21. *Ibid.*, I, 207.
22. *Ibid.*, I, 179.
23. *Ibid.*, I, 178–182.
24. *Ibid.*, I, 191.
25. *Ibid.*, I, 295.
26. *Ibid.*, I, 301.
27. *Ibid.*, I, 303.
28. *Ibid.*, I, 304.
29. *Ibid.*, I, 310–311.
30. *Ibid.*, I, 316–317.
31. *Ibid.*, I, 321–322.
32. *Ibid.*, I, 325.
33. Rose, *The Famous History of Dr. Faustus,* pp. 89–90.
34. *Complete Works,* III, 589.
35. *Ibid.*, III, 590.
36. *Ibid.*, I, 59.
37. *Ibid.*, I, 65.
38. *Ibid.*, I, 69.
39. *Ibid.*, I, 255.
40. *Ibid.*, I, 257.
41. *Ibid.*, I, 259.
42. *Ibid.*, I, 260.
43. *Ibid.*, I, 263.
44. *Ibid.*, III, 530.
45. *Ibid.*, I, 474.

CHAPTER VII

1. For the most part these short stories were collected in *Mosses from an Old Manse* (1846) and *The Snow Image and Other Twice-Told Tales* (1851).
2. *Complete Works,* II, 419.
3. *Ibid.*, II, 418.
4. *Ibid.*, II, 77–78.
5. *Ibid.*, III, 467.
6. *Ibid.*, III, 468.
7. *Ibid.*, III, 469–470.
8. *Ibid.*, II, 197.
9. *Ibid.*, II, 198.
10. *Ibid.*, II, 364.
11. *Ibid.*, II, 377.
12. *Ibid.*, II, 380.
13. *Ibid.*, II, 377.
14. *Ibid.*, II, 365.
15. *Ibid.*, II, 372. Cf. above, p. 40f.
16. *Ibid.*, II, 376.
17. *Ibid.*, II, 374–375.
18. *Ibid.*, II, 377.
19. Benedetto Croce, *Goethe* (New York: Alfred A. Knopf, 1923), p. 56.
20. *Complete Works,* V, 322.
21. *Ibid.*, II, 47.
22. *Ibid.*, II, 50.
23. *Ibid.*, II, 53.
24. *Ibid.*, II, 66.
25. *Ibid.*, II, 137–138.
26. *Ibid.*, II, 116.
27. *Ibid.*, II, 117.
28. *Ibid.*, II, 147.
29. *Ibid.*, II, 524.
30. *Ibid.*, II, 512.
31. *Ibid.*, II, 515.
32. *Ibid.*, II, 529.
33. *Ibid.*, II, 532.
34. *Ibid.*, II, 536.
35. *Ibid.*, III, 461.
36. In "The Procession of Life" Hawthorne offers specific examples of this degradation (*ibid.*, II, 235–252).
37. *Ibid.*, II, 357.
38. *Ibid.*, II, 359–360.
39. *Ibid.*, III, 483.
40. *Ibid.*, III, 495.
41. *Ibid.*, III, 483.
42. *Ibid.*, III, 483.
43. *Ibid.*, III, 494.
44. *Ibid.*, III, 495.
45. *Ibid.*, III, 485.
46. *Ibid.*, III, 491.
47. *Ibid.*, III, 496.
48. *Ibid.*, III, 485.
49. Quoted from *A Discourse on the Moral Tendencies and Results of Human History* (1843), a portion of which appears in *The American Mind,* ed. Harry R. Warfel *et al.* (New York: American Book Company, 1947), II, 1068.

50. *Ibid.,* II, 1067.
51. *Complete Works,* II, 299.
52. *Ibid.,* II, 300.
53. *Ibid.,* II, 455.

CHAPTER VIII

1. This formula derives from Santayana's generalizations on the Faust myth in drama. George Santayana, *Three Philosophical Poets* (Cambridge: Harvard University Press, 1935), p. 149.
2. Lord Raglan, *The Hero* (London: Methuen & Company, Ltd., 1936), p. 277.
3. *Complete Works,* III, 386.
4. *Ibid.,* I, 17.
5. *Ibid.,* V, 79–80.
6. *Ibid.,* V, 94.
7. *Ibid.,* V, 156.
8. *Ibid.,* V, 148–149.
9. *Ibid.,* V, 96.
10. *Ibid.,* V, 97.
11. *Ibid.,* V, 98.
12. *Ibid.,* V, 100.
13. *Ibid.,* V, 208.
14. *Ibid.,* V, 158.
15. See above, pp. 41–42.
16. *Complete Works,* V, 147.
17. *Ibid.,* V, 206.
18. *Ibid.,* V, 205.
19. *Ibid.,* V, 204.
20. *Ibid.,* V, 156.
21. *Ibid.,* V, 164.
22. *Ibid.,* V, 208.
23. *Ibid.,* V, 146.
24. *Ibid.,* V, 143.
25. *Ibid.,* V, 299.
26. *Ibid.,* V, 210.
27. See above, pp. 36–37.
28. See above, pp. 45–47.
29. See above, pp. 40–41.
30. See above, pp. 42–45.
31. *Complete Works,* V, 103–104.
32. *Ibid.,* V, 112.
33. *Ibid.,* V, 199.

34. *Ibid.,* V, 200.
35. *Ibid.,* V, 199.
36. *Ibid.,* V, 193.
37. *Ibid.,* V, 201.
38. Johann Wolfgang von Goethe, *Faust,* trans. John Anster (London: George Routledge, Ltd., n.d.), p. 106. I use this translation of *Faust* because of its popularity and availability in Hawthorne's lifetime. It was the first rendering of *Faust,* Part One, into English (*Dictionary of National Biography,* I, 510), and was published in book form in 1835. Fragments of the translation had appeared earlier in *Blackwood's Edinburgh Magazine* (XXXIX [1820], 235–249). There is ample evidence to prove that Hawthorne's knowledge of German was not sufficient to cope with *Faust* in the original (Stewart, *Nathaniel Hawthorne,* p. 53).
39. Goethe, p. 106.
40. *Complete Works,* V, 222.
41. *Ibid.,* V, 223.
42. *Ibid.,* V, 147.
43. *Ibid.,* V, 174.
44. *Ibid.,* V, 147.
45. *Ibid.,* V, 232.
46. See above, pp. 37–39.
47. *Complete Works,* V, 237.
48. *Ibid.,* V, 237.
49. *Ibid.,* V, 260.
50. *Ibid.,* V, 261.
51. *Ibid.,* V, 263–264.
52. *Ibid.,* V, 265.
53. See above, pp. 45–47, 40–41.
54. *Complete Works,* V, 288.
55. *Ibid.,* V, 285.
56. *Ibid.,* V, 304.
57. *Ibid.,* V, 288.
58. *Ibid.,* V, 118.
59. *Ibid.,* V, 127.
60. *Ibid.,* V, 122.

61. *Ibid.,* V, 124.
62. See above, pp. 41–42.

CHAPTER IX

1. *Complete Works,* III, 42.
2. *Ibid.,* III, 226.
3. *Ibid.,* III, 246.
4. *Ibid.,* III, 368.
5. *Ibid.,* III, 158–159.
6. *Ibid.,* III, 35.
7. *Ibid.,* III, 184.
8. *Ibid.,* V, 400.
9. *Ibid.,* V, 566–567.
10. *Ibid.,* V, 401.
11. *Ibid.,* V, 534.
12. *Ibid.,* V, 500.
13. *Ibid.,* V, 424.
14. *Ibid.,* V, 500.
15. *Ibid.,* V, 534.
16. *Ibid.,* V, 445.
17. *Ibid.,* V, 435.
18. *Ibid.,* V, 584.
19. *Ibid.,* V, 586.
20. *Ibid.,* V, 592.
21. *Ibid.,* V, 365.
22. *Ibid.,* V, 558.
23. *Ibid.,* V, 562.
24. *Ibid.,* VI, 168.
25. *Ibid.,* VI, 46.
26. *Ibid.,* VI, 48–49.
27. *Ibid.,* VI. 50.
28. *Ibid.,* VI, 116.
29. *Ibid.,* VI, 119.
30. *Ibid.,* VI, 132.
31. *Ibid.,* VI, 201.
32. *Ibid.,* VI, 383.
33. *Ibid.,* VI, 247.
34. *Ibid.,* VI, 437.
35. The studies and the sketches for the unfinished romances have been analyzed and partly assembled by Edward H. Davidson in *Hawthorne's Last Phase* (New Haven: Yale University Press, 1949). I am omitting consideration of *The Dolliver*

Romance because its three chapters and trivial preliminary studies afford no evidence of its ultimate design.
36. Davidson, p. 39.
37. *Complete Works,* XIII, 43.
38. *Ibid.,* XIII, 78.
39. *Ibid.,* XIII, 76.
40. *Ibid.,* XIII, 306.
41. *Ibid.,* XIII, 308.
42. *Ibid.,* XIII, 290–291.
43. *Ibid.,* VII, 16.
44. The article appeared in *Scribner's Monthly,* V (1872). It was entitled "Hawthorne's Last Bequest."
45. Lathrop, *A Study of Hawthorne,* p. 272.
46. Davidson, p. 84.
47. *Ibid.,* p. 85.
48. *Ibid.,* p. 112.
49. *Ibid.,* p. 119.
50. *Complete Works,* XI, 232.
51. Goethe, *Faust,* p. 106.
52. *Complete Works,* XI, 233.
53. Goethe, p. 100.
54. *Complete Works,* XI, 240–241.
55. Goethe, p. 101.
56. *Complete Works,* XI, 280.
57. *Ibid.,* XI, 285–286.
58. *Ibid.,* XI, 312.
59. *Ibid.,* XI, 296–297.
60. *Ibid.,* XI, 362.
61. *Ibid.,* XI, 381.
62. *Ibid.,* XI, 395.
63. *Ibid.,* XI, 399.
64. *Ibid.,* XI, 407–408.
65. *Ibid.,* XI, 409.

CHAPTER X

1. *Complete Works,* V, 52.
2. *Ibid.,* I, 26.
3. *Ibid.,* I, 23.
4. *Ibid.,* I, 31.
5. What Toynbee accomplishes by exposition Hawthorne dramat-

ically objectifies in the conflicts of his plots. For instance, the following quotation from the history parallels the latter's belief that the devil incites man into productive action, providing that the challenge of the tempter is courageously met: "In the language of Mythology, when one of God's creatures is tempted by the Devil, God Himself is thereby given the opportunity to recreate the World. By the stroke of the Adversary's trident, all the fountains of the great deep are broken up. The Devil's intervention has accomplished that transition, from static to dynamic, for which God had been yearning ever since the moment when His Yin-state became complete [Adam and Eve in the Garden of Eden before the Fall], but which it was impos-

sible for God to accomplish by Himself, out of His own perfection . . . when once Yin has passed over into Yang, not the Devil himself can prevent God from completing His fresh act of creation. . . ." Toynbee likewise develops the ethico-psychological aspect of the devil-archetype so pervasive in Hawthorne's writings: "Created by God and abandoned to the Devil, he [man] is seen, in the prophet's vision, to be an incarnation of both his Maker and his Tempter, while, in the psychologist's analysis, God and the Devil alike are reduced to conflicting psychic forces in his soul — forces which have no independent existence apart from the symbolic language of Mythology" (*A Study of History*, I, 284–286).

6. *Complete Works*, III, 13.

SELECTIVE BIBLIOGRAPHY

BURR, GEORGE L., ED. *Narratives of the Witchcraft Cases.* New York: Barnes & Noble, Inc., 1914.

BUTLER, E. M. *The Myth of the Magus.* New York: The Macmillan Company, 1948.

CHANDLER, E. L. *A Study of the Sources of the Tales and Romances Written by Nathaniel Hawthorne before 1853.* Smith College Studies in Modern Languages, VII, No. 4. Northampton, Mass.: 1926.

DAVIDSON, EDWARD H. *Hawthorne's Last Phase.* New Haven: Yale University Press, 1949.

GOETHE, JOHANN WOLFGANG VON. *Faust,* trans. John Anster. London: George Routledge, Ltd., n.d.

GOODNIGHT, SCOTT H. *German Literature in American Magazines Prior to 1846.* University of Wisconsin Bulletin No. 203. Madison, 1908.

HAWTHORNE, JULIAN. *Nathaniel Hawthorne and his Wife.* 2 vols. Boston: Houghton, Mifflin and Company, 1884.

HAWTHORNE, NATHANIEL. *The Complete Works of Nathaniel Hawthorne,* with introductory notes by George Parsons Lathrop. 13 vols. Riverside Edition. Boston: Houghton, Mifflin and Company, 1883.

HOFFMAN, E. T. A. *The Devil's Elixir.* London: T. Caldwell, 1824.

JUNG, CARL G. *Contributions to Analytical Psychology,* trans. H. G. and Cary F. Baynes. New York: Harcourt, Brace and Company, 1928.

LATHROP, GEORGE PARSONS. *A Study of Hawthorne.* Boston: Houghton, Mifflin and Company, 1876.

LONGFELLOW, SAMUEL. *Henry Wadsworth Longfellow.* 3 vols. Boston: Houghton, Mifflin and Company, 1883.

MATHER, INCREASE. *Cases of Conscience.* London: Reeves and Turner, 1890.

MATURIN, CHARLES ROBERT. *Melmoth the Wanderer.* 3 vols. London: Charles Bentley, 1892.

MORGAN, BAYARD Q. *A Critical Bibliography of German Literature in English Translation, 1461–1927.* Palo Alto: Stanford University Press, 1938.

PERRY, RALPH BARTON. *Puritanism and Democracy.* New York: The Vanguard Press, 1944.

RAGLAN, LORD. *The Hero.* London: Methuen & Company, 1936.

RAILO, EINO. *The Haunted Castle: A Study of the Elements of English Romanticism.* New York: E. P. Dutton & Company, 1937.

REYNOLDS, GEORGE WILLIAM MACARTHUR. *Faust.* London: George Vickers, 1847.

ROSE, WILLIAM, ED. *The Famous History of Dr. Faustus, 1592–1594.* New York: E. P. Dutton & Company, n.d.

SANTAYANA, GEORGE. *Three Philosophical Poets*. Cambridge: Harvard University Press, 1935.

STEARNS, FRANK P. *The Life and Genius of Nathaniel Hawthorne*. Boston: Richard C. Badger, 1906.

STEWART, RANDALL, ED. *The American Notebooks by Nathaniel Hawthorne*. New Haven: Yale University Press, 1932.

———. *Nathaniel Hawthorne: A Biography*. New Haven: Yale University Press, 1948.

SUMMERS, MONTAGUE. *The Gothic Quest*. London: The Fortune Press, 1938.

THARP, LOUISE. *The Peabody Sisters of Salem*. Boston: Little, Brown and Company, 1950.

TOYNBEE, ARNOLD J. *A Study of History*. 6 vols. London: Oxford University Press, 1939.

WARFEL, HARRY R. *Charles Brockden Brown*. Gainesville: University of Florida Press, 1949.

WRIGHT, THOMAS G. *Literary Culture in New England*. New Haven: Yale University Press, 1920.

INDEX